MW01634533

Cake Decorating

Sugar Art Collection

Marie Sykes & Patricia Simmons

Cake Decorating

Sugar Art Collection

Marie Sykes & Patricia Simmons

CHILD & ASSOCIATES
AN ALL-AUSTRALIAN PUBLISHER

Acknowledgements

The authors and publisher would like to thank the following people for their assistance in the production of this book:

Australian Bakels Pty Ltd	(Pettinice)
A. F. Bambach Pty Ltd	(Wire)
Offray	(Ribbons)
Kenwood Appliances	

Special thanks to Ken Sykes for making cutters, tins and other items.

Warning
Great care should be taken to ensure that cocktail sticks, wires, modelling clay, hobby dough and other non-edible items are used for display purposes only when used in sugarcraft.

Published by
Child & Associates Publishing Pty Ltd,
5 Skyline Place, Frenchs Forest, NSW, Australia, 2086
A wholly owned Australian publishing company
This book has been edited, designed and typeset in Australia by the Publisher
Co-published outside Australia and New Zealand by Merehurst Press
Ferry House, 51-57 Lacy Rd, Putney,
London, SW15 1PR, England
First edition 1989

Photography by Leonard Osbeck and Charles Stoker
Edited by Carol Jacobson
Printed in Singapore by Toppan Printing Co. (S) Pte Ltd
Typesetting processed by Deblaere Typesetting Pty Ltd

National Library of Australia
Cataloguing-in-Publication data

Sykes, Marie.
Sugar art collection.

Includes index.
ISBN 0 86777 182 8.

1. Cake decorating. 2. Sugar art. I. Simmons, Patricia. II. Title.

641.8'653

Dedication

We would like to dedicate this book to Ken Sykes for his untiring help and support over the years.

Half title: *A single-tiered cake covered in delightful Australian fairies dressed in flannel flowers, wattle, Christmas bells, waratahs, and red hot poker or torch lilies. The fairies' wings are made in sheet gelatine and dusted in edible glitter.*

Title: *Two-tiered wedding cake with Singapore orchids. The base of each tier is finished with pure silk organza leaves piped to match the bridal gown.*

Essential equipment for cake decorating: a good quality electric mixer, rolling pin, adequate supply of food colours, brushes, piping tubes and shaping tools as well as ribbons and wire to complete the floral sprays.

Twenty-first birthday cake for twins with a special edge designed for brother and sister.

Contents

Introduction 9

Royal Icing 11
Suspended collar; oriental stringwork; floating bridgework; jewellery; birds

Flowers 19
Aquilegia or columbine; single hibiscus; dwarf azaleas; arum lily; iris; wedding bells; strelitzia or bird of paradise; orange blossom; snowberry and leaves; blue butterfly bush; azaleas; bougainvillea; mock orange blossom; alstroemeria or Peruvian lily; slipper orchid; gum blossom; gloriosa lily; Singapore orchid; wild iris

Moulded Decorations 35
Fairies, gnomes and elves; moulded clowns; squirrel; animals and leaves; rattle; bootee

Sculpture in Low Relief 43

Marshmallow Creme 45

Wired Animals 45

Chocolate 47
To temper chocolate; chocolate leather; coloured chocolate leather; chocolate covering paste; piping chocolate; chocolate leaves; choc gum paste; chocolate decorations

Cocoa Painting 54

Make Your Own Moulds 57

Rice Paper 58

Hobby Dough 59

Airbrushing, Cake Crafting and Figure Piping 61

Cake Sculpture 69

Recipes 71

Step-by-Step Photographs 82

Patterns 89

Index 95

Staggered three-tiered bell-shaped wedding cake topped with floral sprays and decorated with wedding bows.

Introduction

This book, the fourth in the series, has been named *Sugar Art Collection* because it is an assembly of all the wonderful ideas we have collected over five years of travel. Travelling to England, USA, Canada, New Zealand, South Africa and Zimbabwe to demonstrate and teach Australian cake decorating has enabled us to learn many of the methods and styles used in those countries. Upon return we have adapted them to Australian conditions while still retaining their originality and style.

Sugar Art Collection should be used in conjunction with our other books and follows the same style. Special decorations and ideas are first in the book including many new flowers. We also have chapters on airbrushing, cake crafting and cake sculpture. The instructions are in step-by-step format and we have included patterns for most of our designs.

Sugar Art Collection is the perfect companion to our previous books, *Cake Decorating, 101 Cake Decorating Ideas* and *Sugarcraft* and offers the reader exposure to the latest international trends enabling expansion of her or his creative talents.

Note: Only edible products should be used on cakes. Particular attention should be paid to chalk used for colouring. Remember non-toxic does not mean edible.

Scalloped cake, with baby roses and buds, jasmine, embroidery, extension work and lace.

Royal Icing

The suspended collar, upside-down stringwork and floating bridgework are all royal icing specialities practised by expert decorators who have spent years perfecting their own designs and techniques. Following are brief outlines of the basic preparation and design. We must emphasise that practice is essential. Add ⅛ teaspoon of gum arabic to ¾ metric cup of royal icing that has been well beaten and well worked. This will give added strength.

Royal icing flooded plaque with a delightful hand-painted scene.

Special occasion cake with a royal icing suspended collar surrounding a vase of royal icing flowers.

Suspended Collar

The suspended collar is an old technique that was very popular in the late 19th to early 20th centuries. The collar has now been rediscovered by decorators resulting in beautiful and wide variations.

Royal Icing

(for piping supporting strings for collar)

1 egg white
1 1/2 cups (8–9 oz) pure icing (confectioners) sugar
1/8 teaspoon gum arabic or gum tragacanth
1/8 teaspoon glucose

Step 1: Make more than one collar in case one breaks. Position the pattern for the collar under glass or clear perspex to keep it firm; place waxed paper on top of the glass and secure. Using a No. 1 tube and royal icing, pipe the collar outline onto the paper and allow to dry for a short time. Flood with thinned-down royal icing, working around the collar in both directions to complete the circle. This method of joining moist floodwork eliminates a join in the crusted royal icing. Allow to dry under a reading lamp for several hours to give a glossy finish.

Use extreme care when removing the paper—place the collar on a turntable or near a table edge and gently pull the paper with a downward movement.

Step 2: Take four 2.5 cm (1 in) high smooth blocks of wood, sugar cubes, polystyrene or sponge rubber and place at equal distances apart around the top edge of the cake.

Step 3: Place the collar on top of the supports, making sure they are placed evenly under the collar. Using No. 00 or 0 tube commence piping in the centre of the collar. Pipe loops continuously down to form a curtain to the cake top. If threadwork is required, commence piping from the cake top **up** to the edge of the collar.
Note: Loops are easier until you are proficient.

Step 4: Commence piping either loops or threads on the outer edge of collar **in between** the supports. When the icing is dry, carefully remove one support and pipe in the space. Continue in this manner until all supports are removed.

The collar should now be suspended above the cake. Complete the decoration as desired.

Royal icing plaque with a stained glass window in vibrant colours. The design is outlined in chocolate and the top corner features a simple spray of Singapore orchids.

A simple way to use royal icing: pipe children's initials on plain sweet biscuits for great party favourites.

Oriental Stringwork

Oriental stringwork may vary in colour as well as in the length and depth of loops. Use No. 1 writing tube and strengthened royal icing.

Step 1: Turn covered prepared cake upside down onto a smooth surface that is about 1 cm (½ in) smaller than the cake.

Step 2: Mark pattern evenly around the cake.

Step 3: For best results, draw a template first and plan colours. Pipe the first row of loops and allow to dry. Pipe matching loops at base, allow to dry, then turn cake over and finish pipework.

Small piped flowers such as forget-me-nots may be piped where the loops meet. Tiny ejector flowers also make an attractive finish.

Floating Bridgework

Place the covered cake on a stand inside a slightly larger tin. The base of the cake should be approximately 5 mm (¼ in) lower than the upper edge of the tin. Grease the edge or rim of the tin with Copha (solid vegetable oil) and commence piping from a line on the cake to the edge of the tin. Allow to dry.

Pipe dots or tiny scallops where the bridgework meets the cake. This will strengthen the lower edge.

When thoroughly dry, carefully lift the cake straight upwards and then lower it gently on to the prepared board.

Jewellery

Party pieces for children can be made with ribbon, elastic and coloured royal icing. Necklets and bracelets piped on ribbon in colours to match the party scheme are popular and they may also be eaten!

Simple jewellery made from coloured royal icing. These are piped onto ribbon or elastic and make wonderful take-home gifts. (Lou Brough, Zimbabwe)

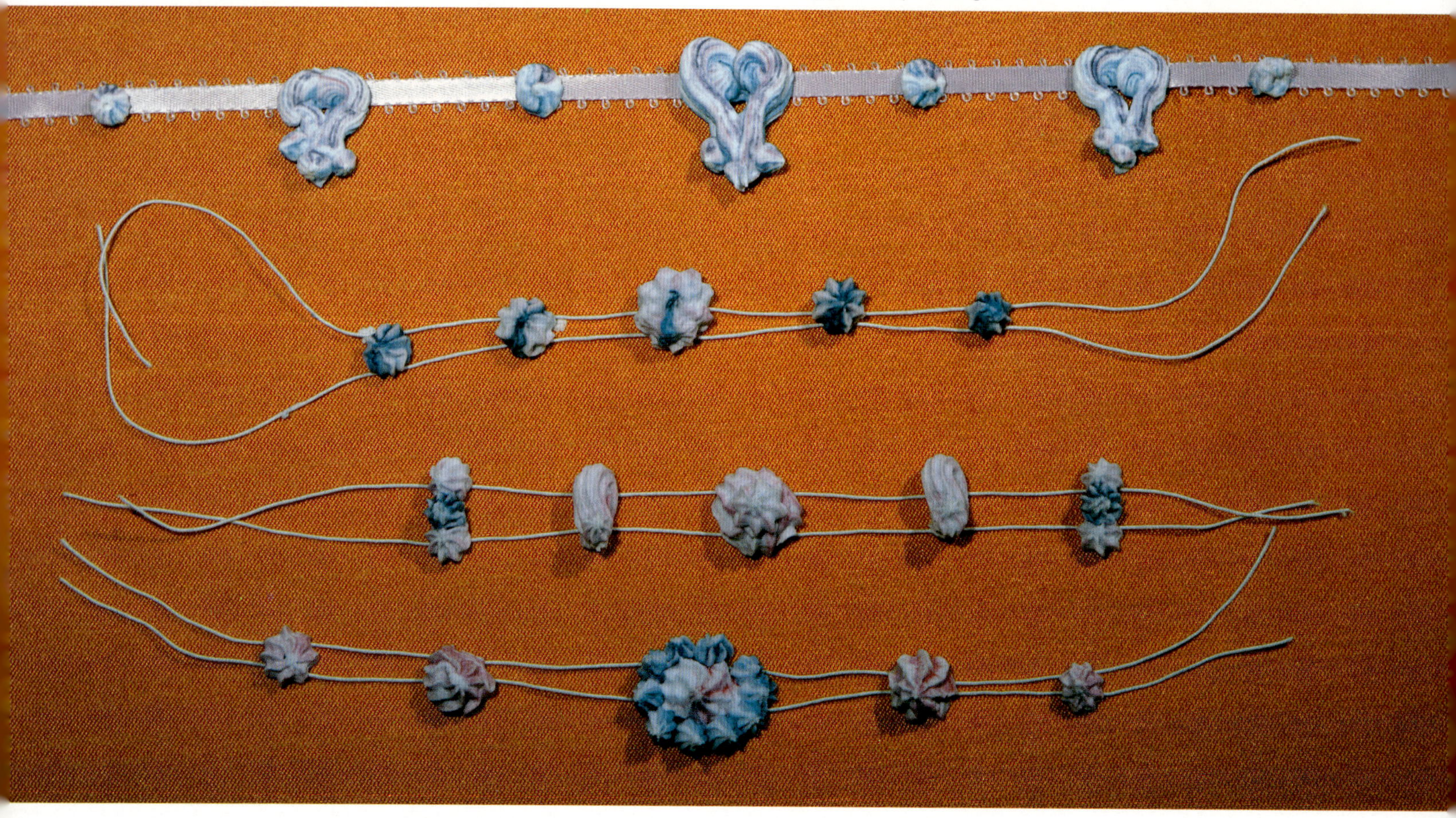

Two-tiered square cake with an orchid spray on each tier. The double frill has been coloured to match the ribbons and flowers.

Birds

Using No. 5 or 8 star tube, place the outline of the bird under a piece of waxed paper. Pipe the outline and fill in the body working towards you. Brush over with a brush moistened in egg white. Allow to crust slightly then overpipe for the wings. Pipe the head and beak last. You may colour the royal icing first, or allow it to dry and paint on the colour later.

These plaques may be done well in advance and allowed to dry. They are popular for children's cakes because they are very simple for beginners and are edible. Children may like to pipe their own decorations in this easy effective method.

Flooded royal icing plaque with Australian parrots and a spray of piped grevillea.

Finely scalloped royal icing plaque showing a small girl opening her Christmas stocking.

Dramatic royal icing plaque in black and white with a silver edge.

Two-tiered wedding cake with pale pink and lemon frangipanis and tiny blossoms.

Flowers

Flowers are the most popular decoration for cakes. Combined with ribbons they form the perfect finishing touch. The style of flowers and the arrangement will depend on the item you are decorating. Once again, practice is essential if your flowers are to be lifelike. Roll the paste very finely to form the delicate petals and keep the colours subtle as some deepen over time. You may find that sometimes it is more practical to alter the natural shape of a flower a little for ease of making.

Single-tiered fiftieth-anniversary cake with daffodils, violets, cream ribbons and yellow embroidery.

Aquilegia or Columbine

These flowers have been cultivated in England for centuries. The colours range from white to pale yellow, pinks to mauves, or dark vivid colour combinations.

Step 1: Wire together a cluster of yellow stamens and bind with florists tape.

Step 2: Cut five small petals as shown, ball the cut edge and cup, turning the edge out. Be sure that the five petals fit around the yellow stamen cluster. Allow to dry.

Step 3: Cut five long petals, ball the cut edges, vein and flute, rounding the tailpiece.

Step 4: Attach the petals to the centrepiece with gum arabic, support the petals with cottonwool and give the tails a slight curve.

Single Hibiscus

Hibiscus grow in temperate to tropical climates. The flowers are large and showy with colours varying from yellow to orange, pink to red, etc. In Hawaii they are used in leis (floral necklaces) to greet people.

Step 1: Mould a long wired stamen tube slightly longer than the petal. Add five stamens to the tip and many cotton stamens part-way down the tube as shown. Allow to dry and add pollen (coloured chalk and fine maize meal).

Step 2: Shape a cone from foil as shown.

Step 3: Cut five petals, vein, ball the cut edges and frill. Moisten one side with gum arabic and place in the foil cup in a spiral, allowing the edges to fall back in a soft curve.

Dwarf Azaleas

Step 1: Cut out pattern as shown. Finger the cut edges, vein, flute and mark a centre vein.

Step 2: Mould a tiny five-sepal calyx the same colour as the flower. Insert fine wire and moisten the inside with gum glue.

Step 3: Place the flower in the calyx, carefully firming the centre.

Step 4: Add five fine stamens in the same colour as the flower and tip brown. Add a stigma which is tipped green.

Step 4: Moisten the base of the flower and add stamen tube. Support until dry.

Step 5: To make buds, shape a piece of green moulding paste, into a hollow cone. Cut five sepals and add wire. Add a second calyx to the base as shown.

Step 6: Cut two petals, shape the same as for the flower, fold into an S shape and place into the soft calyx. Allow to dry.

Leaves are green and veined. Sizes vary from very small to large.

Birthday cake with three deep red hibiscus in front of a moulded fan. The side is decorated with a brush painting of a hibiscus.

Arum Lily

The arum lily is a large white trumpet flower with large leaves that are heavily veined.

Step 1: Mould a tube about 3 cm (1¼ in) long, tapering to the top. Allow to dry.

Step 2: Brush with a mixture of fine maize meal and yellow chalk for a pollen effect.

Step 3: Cut a shape as shown. Ball the cut edges and pinch the tip. Roll the shape around the tube, moistening with gum arabic.

Iris

Iris are beautiful showy flowers that bloom in white, yellow, rich blues, mauves, deep bronze, etc., with colourful contrasts.

Step 1: Cut three lower petals and insert wire. Ball the cut edges, vein and frill and set in a deep curve. Moisten a strip with egg white or gum glue and sprinkle pollen on the surface.

Step 2: Cut three small inside petals and shape as shown. Take a nick out of the blunt end and frill slightly. Fasten to the three lower petals as shown.

Step 3: Cut three upper petals and insert wire. Ball the cut edges, vein and frill and set face downwards over a gentle curve. Allow to dry.

Step 4: Colour as desired. Wind a small strip of florists tape at base of each petal where wire joins.

Step 5: Bind the three upper petals together and then the three lower petals. Bind the two sets into a double triangle. Adjust the petals with tweezers if necessary.

Wedding Bells

Wedding bells are tiny pink double flowers. The buds are round green balls with the opening marked, and a tiny ovary at the base. Leaves are elongated and heavily veined.

Step 1: Mould a small teardrop and hollow out to form a cone.

Step 2: Cut five shallow petals; ball the edges and cup the tops. Insert fine wire and five fine yellow stamens. Allow to dry.

Step 3: Cut a five-petal shape as shown. Ball the petals and moisten the centre. Insert the prepared dried centre into the middle of the five-petal shape. Cup the petals around the dried centre. Allow to dry.

Step 4: Mould or paint a green calyx.

Strelitzia or Bird of Paradise

Strelitzia, a close relative of the banana family, originated in South Africa where it is known as the crane flower. Two brilliant peacock blue petals are surrounded by five to seven bright orange sepals.

Step 1: Cut nine fine wires about 12.5 cm (5 in) long. Cut and wire seven orange sepals. Finger the cut edges, vein and pinch lightly. Centre the vein at the back of the sepal.

Step 2: Lay to dry in required positions as shown.

Step 3: Cut two or three peacock blue petals as shown. Insert wire for the stem.

Step 4: Using a ball tool, smooth edges and shape the petal. Mark the centre vein and tilt the head slightly back. Allow to dry.

Step 5: To make up, wire together two sepals, one flower and then two additional sepals to make the first floret. Allow to dry.

Step 6: Wire together one sepal, one flower and then two additional sepals to make the second floret. Allow to dry.

Step 7: Tape together the first floret and then the second floret along a firm wire extended 5 cm (2 in) beyond the flower and level with the other end.

Step 8: Cover the wires at the base of the flower with Pettinice or rolled covering paste.

Step 9: Cut a green pod shape and texture the surface with a corn husk. Place in position with the point at the front as shown. The back should be tapered to the thick stem. Stems can be moulded separately and placed under the flower or moulded over double heavy wire. Dust the pod lightly with a mixture of browns and reds to reduce the effect of the bright green.

Orange Blossom

A typical wedding flower of yesteryear, orange blossom has a strong perfume and a very waxy appearance.

Step 1: Take a piece of moulding paste about the size of a small pea and mould into a tear drop shape.

Step 2: Hollow the centre to form a hollow cone and cut the top edge into five equal parts for petals. Mitre the edges and turn the petals back.

Step 3: Roll out a small piece of moulding paste approximately 2 x 1.5 cm (3/4 x 1/2 in). Fringe one side with a fine sharp blade. Wrap the piece around a green tipped stamen; moisten the base and place inside the flower. Allow to dry. This represents a fringe of stamens.

Step 4: Tint the tips of the fringe with lemon, yellow or green chalks.

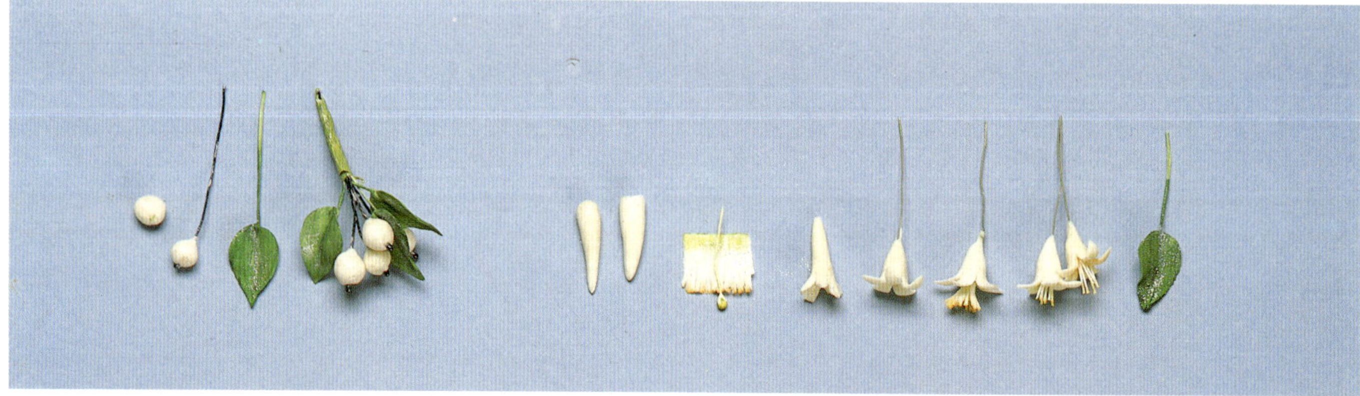

Snowberry and Leaves

Snowberry consists of small clusters of white berries that hang like mothballs during the winter, with an oval pointed leaf. Hybrids are now grown in pale pink and red.

Step 1: Mould a small piece of white moulding paste into a pea-sized ball. Pull a black stamen through the centre, leaving the black tip protruding.

Step 2: Mould leaves as shown in pattern.

Mould numerous berries and leaves. Group three to five berries together, bind with florists tape and add leaves.
Snowberry makes a novel filler flower.

Opposite: *Oval birthday cake with strelitzia and baby's breath, satin ribbon, lace and extension work.*

Blue Butterfly Bush

This unusual small two-tone blue flower resembles a butterfly. A shrub in full flower resembles a cloud of blue butterflies.

Step 1: Mould a small green calyx on a fine wire and allow to dry.

Step 2: Cut or mould one pair of upper wing petals. Ball and shape and place in the dry calyx.

Step 3: Cut or mould one pair of lower wing petals slightly larger than the upper wings. Ball and shape and place in the dry calyx, overlapping slightly at base of the upper petals.

Step 4: Cut or mould one teardrop-shaped petal for the body. Ball and shape and place in the centre between the wing petals.

Step 5: Prepare five very fine stamens and one a little thicker for the pistil. Curve stamens and pistil and place between the top petals and body as shown. Dust the wings with pale blue and use a slightly deeper colour for the body. The leaves are small, clearly veined with a serrated edge.

Azaleas

Azaleas are popular because of their floral abundance and the variety of colours from deep reds, pink, salmon, yellow to white, including variegated colours. Sizes vary from dwarf to regular and single to double blooms.

Step 1: Cut five petals and finger the cut edges. Vein, flute and mark a centre vein. Moisten the back of each petal and place four in a small foil cup in a spiral shape as shown. The fifth petal is placed alongside the fourth, to form a circle on the outer edges.

Step 2: Insert five fine stamens and one stigma the same colour as the flower. The stigma has a tiny green ball on the tip and the stamens are brown tipped. Allow to dry.

Step 3: Mould a small five-sepal calyx. Insert wire, moisten with gum glue and add to the base of the flower. Allow to dry.

Step 4: Using a fine brush, paint small marks of a darker tone on the fifth petal and a few overflowing marks on to the next touching petals.

Oval plaque with magenta bougainvillea and leaves, finished with lace.

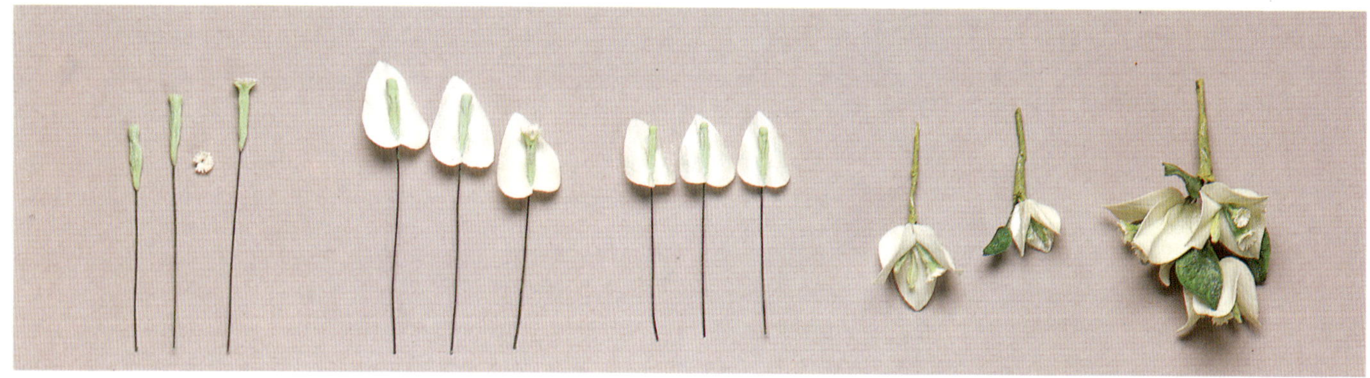

Bougainvillea

Bougainvillea, originally from South America, has about eighteen species and is very showy. It comes in a riot of brilliant colours, with bracts surrounding three insignificant flowers.

Prepare three centres as described below and allow to dry. Attach to three pieces of fine medium covered wire, coloured green.

1st centre: Cover approximately 2–2.5 cm (¾–1 in) wire with small tube of paste in the desired colour. Roll to shape and leave a tiny bud on the top. Touch with white colour and pinch five veins along the tube.

2nd centre: Repeat as above, but hollow the tip with a fine needle or toothpick. Cut five tiny sepals. Touch with white, cream or lemon and pinch five veins along the tube.

3rd centre: Repeat as for the second centre, but open the sepals wide enough to hold the tiny flower below.

Flower: Take a tiny piece of paste in cream or pale lemon and cut with a tiny cutter, or use a very tiny hollow cone and fringe the edges. Keep the flower as flat as possible and attach to the sepals with egg white, gum arabic or paste glue. Allow to dry.

Bracts: Roll paste as finely as possible and cut three bracts in desired shade. The bracts should match the colour of the flower tube.

Vein the bracts and pinch along the back. Place one dry flower on bract and secure with paste glue. Fold the base of the bract around the base of the flower.

Repeat for the remainder of the bracts and flowers.

Tape three bracts together with brown or green florists tape or Stemtex and allow to dry.

Spray: Arrange several sizes of flowers and numerous leaves to form each spray.

Two-tiered oval wedding cake on perspex boards and columns. Each tier holds a spray of white bougainvillea.

Mock Orange Blossom

Mock orange is a small white flowering shrub with flowers resembling orange blossom. The flowers each have four petals, four sepals and numerous fine yellow stamens. The buds are cupped with much larger leaves.

Step 1: Mould a four-sepal green calyx, insert wire, firm on and allow to dry.

Step 2: Cut and mould four petals with the edge curving outwards. Nip a small piece from the top edge on one or two petals. Moisten the back of the lower tip of the petals with gum arabic and set in opposite pairs. Firm into the dried calyx using a modelling stick. Give the petals a little lift or curve, do not set straight.

Step 3: Place a tiny piece of moulding paste in the centre of the flower and add numerous pale yellow stamens. Allow to dry.

Alstroemeria or Peruvian Lily

Alstroemeria are showy flowers that are natives of central and South America. They grow in vibrant colours of orange, red and yellow, although hybrids are grown in pale and deep pinks.

There are many varieties and shapes in this particular lily and the one illustrated has been altered slightly to suit decorating purposes. They are very unusual and striking flowers suitable for most types of decoration.

Step 1: Bind together six long stamens and one pistil with florists tape. Add a very small ball of moulding paste to the tip of each stamen. When dry, colour the small balls a reddish brown and the stamen cottons pink.

Step 2: Cut three small pointed petals (as shown). Vein, attach wire and allow to dry.

Step 3: When dry, lightly streak two petals in the same reddish brown as the stamens. Lightly dust the tip with green and colour the rest of the petal pink. Dust the third petal a slightly deeper pink without streaks.

Step 4: Bind together the two streaked petals so that they are slightly overlapping and are in the 11 and 12 o'clock positions. Bind the pink petal in the 6 o'clock position using florists tape.

Step 5: Prepare some cottonwool to support the petals made in the next stage.

Step 6: Cut three large round petals. Stretch the edges, vein, moisten with gum arabic and attach to the centre petals.

Step 7: Place the petals in the 3, 9 and 12 o'clock positions. Allow the petals to curl back slightly and support with prepared cottonwool until thoroughly dry.

Step 8: Dust the tips of the outer petals with green and colour the rest pale pink.

Opposite: *Oval twenty-first birthday cake with piped scallop trim and superb slipper orchid spray.*

Slipper Orchid

The slipper orchid is one of many varieties in the orchid family and is often called miller's daughter. There are so many colour combinations in this species that it becomes the personal choice of the decorator. When making this orchid, artistic licence has been taken to create a soft appearance. In its natural form the slipper orchid is very shiny. If this is desired, spray with cooking spray, or briefly hold over steam. The natural column is very thick and heavy and we have modified it for decorating purposes. The orchid illustrated here is called miller's daughter.

Step 1: Mould a slim flat bean approximately 2.5 cm (1 in) long around wire. Allow to dry.

Step 2: Roll out paste but not paper thin. Cut the shape as per pattern. This may be done by hand, however the cutter method is much easier.

Step 3: Place in the palm of the hand, thin all edges, but do not alter the shape.

Step 4: Curl in No. 1 using a fine cocktail stick.

Step 5: Glue down toe on one side and fold over until the sides overlap. Smooth over the seam carefully.

Step 6: Gently stroke the centre of the lip outwards.

Step 7: Place the foundation on the slipper seam. Glue, roll No. 2 inwards to hide the seam; pinch down centre front to form vein.

Step 8: Mould the column in a circle or heart shape. Fold over your finger to curl slightly. Allow to dry.

Step 9: Cut a circle of foil and form into a slight concave cup shape. Push a hole through the centre. Rest the foil over the top of a glass tumbler.

Step 10: Cut out the lateral petals. Thin the edges without stretching and frill gently.

Step 11: Pinch down the centre back of each petal to make the main veins, then add numerous other veins.

Step 12: Arrange the petals in the correct positions around the hole in the foil.

Step 13: Cut out the side wing petals. Vein the petals as above. Glue the wing petals to the lateral petals and place the wired slipper throat through centre of the wing petal.

Step 14: If required, support the petals with cottonwool or tissues until dry. Colour as desired.

Above: *Large birthday cake with a magnificent slipper orchid. The edge is finished with a stippled border touched with gold dust.*

Gum Blossom

Gum blossom is the flower of various members of the Eucalypt family, and blooms in shades of reds, pinks, salmon, apricot and cream.

Step 1: Loosely wind about 3 metres (6 ft) of coloured cotton around a small cylinder.

Step 2: Remove cotton from cylinder and wire into bunches. Cut cotton to form tufts of stamens.

Step 3: Mould a small hollow cone, insert wired cotton stamens. Firm the core on to the wire and allow to dry.

Step 4: Brush ends of cotton with gum arabic and dip into yellow non-toxic chalk.

Step 5: Mould gum leaves, add wire and allow to dry. Add to the spray.

Gloriosa Lily

Also called the flame lily, the gloriosa lily is a very striking tropical flower from Africa and is the national flower of Zimbabwe. It has claw-like leaves with bright yellow and red blossoms changing to orange and claret with age.

Step 1: Cut six fine wires about 6 cm (2¼ in) long for stamens. Mould and bind all wires. Using yellow moulding paste make six antler tips and attach to the end of each wire. Allow to dry.

Step 2: Take a rounded piece of green moulding paste about 12 x 6 mm (½ x ¼ in) and thread it on to a piece of fine wire about 15 cm (6 in) long. Leave 4 cm (1½ in) at one end for the pistil.

Step 3: For the pistil, mould a tiny piece of green moulding paste around the pistil end of the wire and cut into three pieces. Make three vertical indentations around the pod. Insert the prepared tipped stamens as shown.

Step 4: Take a small roll of yellow moulding paste and shape into a petal as shown. Place on top of a larger piece of red moulding paste. Roll lengthwise and cut out six petals. Flute the edges, pinch the centre veins and wire each petal. Set each petal with a curl and allow to dry on its side.

Step 5: To assemble, gently curve the stamens away from the base stem.

Step 6: Bind each wire close to the petal with a tiny piece of tape. Place the petals evenly around the long main stem and bind fully. (Petals curve away from the green pod.)

Step 7: Dust the base of the petals with green chalk.

Engagement cake with pink tiger lilies and other small flowers.

Singapore Orchid

The Singapore orchid, from the genus *Dendrobium*, is used often in wedding bouquets and floral arrangements. The illustrated bloom is a creamy colour and it has a pale lime green tongue. Buds and new flowers are also pale lime green. They also grow in various reds, pinks and mauves.

Step 1: Mould a small column as shown, shape, moisten and insert the wire. Allow to dry before commencing the next step.

Step 2: Cut the throat and pinch the centre with tweezers as shown. Stretch the edges and frill slightly. Cup the lobes to stand up. Moisten and attach to column. Allow to dry.

Step 3: Cut out two lower petals. Stretch the edges, vein and attach to the throat as shown. Allow to dry in a bed of cornflour (cornstarch).

Step 4: Cut out the centre top petal and the two upper side petals. Stretch the edges, vein, wire and curve slightly for a natural look. Allow to dry. Wrap a tiny strip of florists tape around the wire immediately below the petal.

Step 5: Take completed lower section (up to step 3) and attach the wired upper petals, placing the centre one first, then the two side petals and bind the whole with parafilm.

Buds are boatshaped and lime green. Wire a few and add them to the spray.

Wild Iris

Wild iris are large white flowers with mauve and orange-yellow markings. They are evergreens and in warm weather produce blooms on long stems. The wild iris is a native of South Africa.

Step 1: Place the stem wire in a small ball of paste. Roll out as fine as possible. Cut to shape as shown.

Step 2: Cut down one third of petal, ball the edge and shape with fingers and vein on top. Dry as shown. Prepare three of these to make stigmas. When dry colour light mauve.

Step 3: For the petals, lace wire into small ball of paste and roll and cut to shape as shown.

Step 4: Reverse and ball the edges. Place on veiner and heavy vein on reverse side. Prepare three petals. When dry touch up the centres with small dots and strokes of brown. Allow to dry.

Step 5: For the sepals, insert wire into a ball of paste and roll and cut to shape as shown.

Step 6: Ball the edges to stretch into the desired shape. Prepare three sepals. When dry, paint a bright yellow splash three-quarters of the way up the petal from the base. Add a touch of brown at the top to emphasise the sharp outline. Allow to dry.

Step 7: Take the three mauve stigmas and bind together with Stemtex or florists tape.

Step 8: Place the three petals in alternate spaces and bind together.

Step 9: Place the sepals behind the mauve stigmas and bind together.

Moulded decoration with floral adornment and airbrushed colour. The flowers are dusted with petal dust.

Moulded Decorations

Once the basic shapes have been learned, moulding is simple and can be done by children. Moulded decorations make a delightful change from traditional flowers and give the decorator more scope in the design. Marzipan can be used as well as moulding paste and there are a wide variety of speciality tools available. However many household utensils can be adapted for use in moulding. For children's items, use bright colours to catch their eyes.

Collection of fairies, gnomes and elves, hand-moulded and sprinkled with glitter.

Fairies, Gnomes and Elves

Body and Head

Step 1: Make a mould from a tiny plastic doll's head. Allow to dry. When the mould is set, use it to make as many dolls' heads as required for your fairy scene. Insert toothpicks or firm wire into the neck. When dry, colour the face with chalk and use a fine paint brush for detail.

Step 2: For each body, mould a rounded carrot shape, in proportion to the size of the head.

Step 3: Split the narrow point of the carrot for the legs and cut an arm on either side of the thicker part, making sure the proportion is correct.

Step 4: Shape the arms and legs, flattening the base for feet and the base of arms for the hands.

Step 5: Bend the arms at elbows and legs at the back of the knees. Set the arms and legs of each body at varied angles. Firm wire may be inserted in one leg to make the figure stand up. Set some in sitting positions for variety. Ballerinas, skaters, etc. may be made using the same method.

Step 6: Place the heads on the dolls and leave them to set in varied positions. Dress as desired.

Wings

Wings can be made from very finely rolled moulding paste (transparent), rice paper, tulle, stiffened cotton net or sheet gelatine.

Cut one pair of wings as shown. The wings may be finished with edible glitter (see below) and the fairies may also be moulded in Hobby Dough (see page 59). For gnomes and elves, use the same body and dress as desired. On page 35 we have illustrated Australian bush flower fairies made from the same pattern.

To Make Edible Glitter

Place 2 tablespoons of cold water in a double saucepan and sprinkle 60 g (2 oz) gum arabic on top. Heat gently, stirring until dissolved. Colour as desired. Strain through a piece of muslin or cheesecloth and brush onto a clean biscuit tray. Place the tray in a cool oven 140°C (275°F/ Gas 1) to dry. When dry, scrape the tray with a knife and flake the glitter between the fingers. Store in an airtight jar.

Moulded Clowns

Step 1: Using half moulding paste and half rolled covering paste mould a sausage shape 9 x 2.5 cm (3½ x 1 in) for the body. Mould it a little thicker at one end.

Step 2: Cut the sausage in two at the thick end to form the legs. Twist the legs so that cut side is underneath. Form the body into a sitting position.

Step 3: Mould two hands and push a rounded stick into each wrist.

Step 4: Using black or brown moulding paste, mould a sausage shape 2 x 2.5 cm (¾ x 1 in) for two large shoes. Cut in two and push a rounded cocktail stick into each. Push shoes into each leg using egg white or gum arabic.

Step 5: Mould a sausage shape 12 x 2.5 cm (4½ in) for the arms. Cut in two and place in position with egg white or gum arabic.

Step 6: Cut a round flat piece 5 cm (2 in) in diameter for the collar and frill the edge. Cut three small pieces for hat, hands and head.

Step 7: Mould an egg shape for the head. Attach to the body with a cocktail stick and egg white or gum arabic. Allow to dry.

Step 8: Using royal icing and No. 1 writing tube, pipe the hair or use a clay gun.

Step 9: Mould a cone-shaped hat. Slightly hollow out the wide end and place on the head.

Step 10: Decorate the face with eyes, brows, nose and mouth. Add pompoms. Support the clown with cottonwool until dry.

Animals and Leaves

Squirrel

Step 1: Roll a piece of cream rolled covering paste into a sausage shape approximately 7 x 1.2 cm (2¾ x ½ in).

Step 2: Squeeze one end gently to form a nose. Pinch up the ears and make small indentations for the eyes. Bend the head slightly forward.

Step 3: Bend half the remaining paste up behind the head. Thin the edges slightly and bend back a little to form a tail. With pointed scissors snip the front body under the head to form front paws. Snip the lower front to form back paws. Allow to dry.

Step 4: Paint the body with brown colouring and the eyes with deep blue or green.

Echidna or Hedgehog

Step 1: Make a ball of rolled covering paste and thin one side to form a long pointed nose. Pinch up ears and make indentations for eyes.

Step 2: With pointed scissors snip the body in rows to form spines, starting the first row behind the ears and continuing over the whole body. Allow to dry.

Step 3: Paint the body with dark brown colouring and the eyes with deep blue or green.

Acorns

Step 1: Using caramel brown colouring tint some moulding paste a beige colour. Make several cones in sizes from 2–3 cm (¾-1 ¼ in) long. Round the wide end of each cone and pinch up a small tip on the point.

Step 2: With a small piece of moulding paste make a shallow rounded cup to fit onto the thicker rounded end of each cone. Attach to the cone and wire. Allow to dry.

Step 3: Paint the cone, base and wire with caramel brown colouring with a little black added. Streak each cone lightly with a slightly darker colour.

Undeveloped Acorns

Step 1: Place very small balls of beige moulding paste onto a piece of thin foam. Indent the centre of each with the flat end of a bamboo skewer. Allow to dry.

Step 2: Attach to wire with a little royal icing. Paint the wire and balls with dark brown colouring.

Oak Leaves

Step 1: With moulding paste, make a small bud shape and wire with heavy wire. Allow to dry. Paint the bud and wire with dark brown colouring.

Step 2: Colour some moulding paste a bright yellowish green using a mixture of green and yellow colouring. Take a piece of fine wire, moisten and place into a ball of the paste. Roll out finely.

Step 3: Using the required leaf pattern, cut out the leaves. Finger the cut edges and vein. Dry in different shapes, small leaves with the side and top edges curving up, larger leaves flatter with only the top edge curling up. Most sprays require about six to nine leaves. Allow to dry.

Step 4: If necessary, paint the leaves with a mixture of yellow and green colouring. New oak leaves are bright light green, gradually darkening to deep green.

Step 5: To assemble, use a dark brown bud as the centre and arrange five or more leaves of different sizes around the bud. Twist the wires onto heavy wire and turn leaves outward at right angles. Bend wires on acorns at right angles and arrange in leaves with undeveloped acorns.

Branch

Roll a piece of beige moulding paste into a thin sausage shape approximately 15 cm (6 in) long. Snip at an angle about one third along the sausage and bend slightly. Roughen three-quarters of the surface with a toothpick. Allow to dry. Paint with dark brown colouring.

Mouse

Step 1: Make a small ball of rolled covering paste and narrow one end to form a nose. Pinch up pointed ears and make indentations for eyes.

Step 2: Shape a thin roll of paste to form a tail and attach to the rear of the body with a little egg white or water. Allow to dry. Paint the body with grey or light brown colouring and the eyes with blue.

Rattle

Cut a ping-pong ball in half and cut about 2 mm (1⁄10 inch) from each half. Flatten out a ball of paste about the size of a marble. Place inside one half ball and work until fine and thin and well fitting inside the half ball. Using any small cutter, cut out shapes while still inside the half ball. Make the other half in the same way. Cut out handle and let all three pieces dry. Make sure the handle is no thicker than 2 mm (1⁄10 in). Remove the shapes from the half balls.

Pipe a row of royal icing around the ring of one dried half. Place over the cut out ring in the handle, making sure it is centred. Wipe away any excess icing. Turn upside down and rest the handle on something small (e.g. a matchbox).

COURTESY SELMA ALLEN, SYDNEY, AUSTRALIA

Pipe the second half and place on top. Holding by the two halves, check that you have a round ball. Allow to dry.

Using No. 1 writing tube, pipe a small shell around the base of the top half and handle and also all around the side of the handle. Pipe forget-me-nots over the top of one half ball and the handle. Allow to dry and repeat on the other side. Pipe in different colours to the moulding paste.

Bootee

Mould two logs about 2.5–4 cm (1–1½ in) long and 1.2–2 cm (½–¾ in) high and 1.2 cm (½ in) wide. Squeeze in slightly just above the middle of the log and round off both ends. Flatten the top and bottom. Prick the bottom and allow to dry. Using No. 1 writing tube, pipe straight lines close together along the top from halfway towards the toes (the long end). After this has set a little, prick down each line with the pointed end of a toothpick. This gives the effect of knitted stocking stitch. Place on a cotton reel. (The reel may be turned about without touching.)

Using No. 5 star tube, pipe around the sides meeting the top piping. Pipe the second row in between the shells. Continue until the sides are covered. Allow to dry.

Pipe the top in a circle, each row on top of the last. Build up as high as required.

Place a bow in front, insert a ribbon around the base of circle. When completely dry, flood inside circle.

Above: *Delicately shaded twins' christening cake with a hand-moulded crib, hand-painted decoration and sprays of escallonia and double eriostemon. The side has fine embroidery and lace.*

Opposite: *Tiny piped bootees and moulded rattle with floral and ribbon sprays. Both are on plaques that have been delicately shaded.* (Joan Jack)

Rolled covering paste plaque with three-dimensional design made by building up the design and then covering it with coloured moulding paste.

Sculpture in Low Relief

Sculpture in low relief is a three dimensional style of decorating. Figures are built up with rolled covering paste and then covered with moulding paste to make attractive decorations. The sculpture may be simple or complicated. Colour plays a very important part in this style of decorating.

Australian birds and flowers in a three-dimensional sculpture on a rolled covering paste plaque.

Step 1: Prepare a plaque of rolled covering paste or moulding paste and allow to dry. Turn the plaque over at intervals to make sure that it is thoroughly dry. Trace the selected design on the plaque with a non-toxic pencil. Using rolled covering paste, mould the shape over the pencilled outline.

Step 2: Pad out the shape of the head and cheeks, etc., then the neck, torso, waist and skirt. Use rolled covering paste to build the skirt with extra folds for fullness. Mould and place the shoes in position.

Step 3: Roll out a small quantity of flesh-coloured moulding paste and cover the head and neck. For the ear, make a small half-round cut into the soft icing. Lift the ear so that it will stand up slightly.

Step 4: Colour the moulding paste for the dress and roll out the bodice and skirt. Cover the figure, turning the side edges under. Cover the shoes.

Step 5: Roll out a narrow piece of moulding paste for the ribbon around the waist and the bow at the back. Place in position.

Step 6: Shape a small roll of flesh-coloured paste for the arms. Flatten one end at the shoulder, bend the elbow and cut out a thumb and four fingers at the other end. Allow to dry. Cover the arm with a long sleeve of rolled moulding paste frilled at the shoulder. Place the arm in position.

Step 7: Mould a few small flowers for the girl's posy and hair. Place in position. The background may be chalked and the leaves and flowers may be painted, moulded or piped.

Square christening cake with a flooded design on a frilled plaque.

Marshmallow Creme

2 cups (500 g/1 lb) crystal sugar
60 g (2 oz) gelatine
1 ¼ cups (250 ml/8 fl oz) water
pinch of cream of tartar

Combine ingredients and boil for 15 minutes. Pour into a jar when just warm and allow to stand for 24 hours before use. Pipe the outline of selected design in royal icing use No. 1 or 2 writing tube.

Melt the marshmallow crème in a container over hot water. When melted, colour and place a small quantity in a paper bag and fill the design. Keep designs simple for the best effect.

Right: *The decoration on this child's birthday cake is made by filling a piped outline with melted marshmallow.*

Wired Animals

Step 1: Mould each half of the animal and allow to dry. Build up reverse side to match.

Step 2: Build up muscle and allow to dry.

Step 3: Paint over with thin royal icing and allow to dry.

Step 4: Paint pattern on skin. Finish mane and tail.

Step 5: Mould two front legs. Mould mirror pair.

Step 6: Mould two hind legs. Mould mirror pair.

Three-tiered wedding cake with roses. The bridge was made using moulded cutter pieces (see page 82).

Chocolate

Most decorators at some time try their hand at chocolate work and find it a very satisfying pastime. The more adventurous of these decorators have experimented until we now have moulding chocolate, sometimes called chocolate leather, rolled chocolate for covering cakes and piping chocolate. Brief instructions for each is given here, plus recipes for the interested decorator to experiment with and pursue this exotic medium.

Pure chocolate or couverture is smooth and glossy with a flavour which is superior to that of compounded chocolate (also called bakers chocolate or summer coating). Because of the high content of cocoa butter, pure chocolate needs to be tempered before use (see following page) whereas compounded chocolate is easier to handle, especially for beginners.

Moulded figures in coloured chocolate are placed on individual boards. The figures are dressed using choc gum paste.

To Temper Chocolate

Grate the chocolate into a double saucepan. Using a confectionery thermometer, heat to 38–46°C (100–115°F), stirring constantly. Remove from the heat and stand the top pan in cold water to bring the temperature down to 27–28°C (80–82°F), stirring well. The chocolate is now ready for use. For milk or white chocolate use 1°C (2°F) lower temperature in each case.

Chocolate Leather

(chocolate moulding paste)

150 g (5 oz) compounded chocolate, broken into small pieces
½ cup (125 ml/4 fl oz) glucose or corn syrup

Melt the compounded chocolate in a double saucepan over warm water then add the glucose at room temperature. Stir until blended. When firm, knead well and wrap in plastic and seal in an airtight container. This mixture may be used to mould flowers, animals, etc.

Coloured Chocolate Leather

Add powdered colouring or special oil-based colours and oil-based flavourings to white chocolate leather for moulding flowers, fruits, etc.

This doll is made from white chocolate and dressed in choc gum paste.

Chocolate Covering Paste

This is made by combining two different batches of ingredients.

Batch No. 1
125 g (4 oz) white compounded chocolate

125 g (4 oz) milk compounded chocolate
¼ cup (65 ml/2 fl oz) glucose or corn syrup

Melt the compounded chocolate in a double saucepan over hot tap water then add the glucose at room temperature. Stir until smooth and well combined and spread on a plastic sheet. Set aside.

Batch No. 2
¼ cup (30 g/1 oz) good quality cocoa
1 kg (2 lb) pure icing (confectioners) sugar
1 tablespoon instant coffee
4 tablespoons hot water
½ cup (125 ml/4 fl oz) glucose
1 teaspoon vanilla essence
good pinch salt
2 tablespoons Copha or solid white vegetable shortening

Sieve the cocoa and icing sugar together in a large bowl.

Dissolve the coffee in the hot water then add the glucose, vanilla essence, salt and vegetable shortening. Heat gently until the shortening is just melted.

Pour the liquids into the dry ingredients and stir until thick. Bind together gently by hand. Turn on to a board lightly sprinkled with pure icing (confectioners) sugar and knead until smooth.

Place Batch No. 1 on top of Batch No. 2 and knead the two together. Add more pure icing (confectioners) sugar if necessary to make a smooth workable consistency. Wrap in plastic until ready for use.

Spray a little cooking spray on the bench first, then dust lightly with pure icing (confectioners) sugar. Brush a thin layer of thinned-down apricot jam (jelly) or piping gel over the cake and cover with the chocolate paste in the usual manner.

Delicate plaque made by piping the outline in chocolate and then flooding with royal icing. An arum lily spray is resting on the right.

Piping Chocolate

Add 2–3 drops of glycerine to 1 cup (250 ml/8 fl oz) melted compounded chocolate. Mix well. Use to pipe fine lines on petit fours, etc.

Note: Piping gel is also a good substitute for glycerine.

Chocolate Leaves

Paint melted compounded chocolate on clean rose or violet leaves, etc. Allow to dry and gently peel off the leaf. Chocolate leaves can be used to decorate ice cream desserts. or cream cakes, etc.

Choc Gum Paste

Mix together ⅔ quantity of chocolate covering paste (see page 48) and ⅓ quantity of gum paste (see page 74). Use piping gel to attach.

Note: Depending on the consistency required, you may use ½ quantity of chocolate paste and gum paste.

COURTESY SHIRLEY JACKSON, MICHIGAN, USA

Chocolate Decorations

For the best possible results, use compounded chocolate. This is available in dark, milk and white. Use only oil-based food colours in the chocolate. To melt the chocolate, place in a glass or china bowl and stand in hot tap water. **DO NOT OVERHEAT**.

If you stand your bowl in an electric frypan set at the lowest heat and half filled with water you will be able to work with the chocolate for a longer period.

COURTESY SELMA ALLEN, SYDNEY, AUSTRALIA

Flowers

Flowers can be made from moulds (obtained from plastic flowers). Separate the petals of the flowers and wash with soap. **DO NOT USE DETERGENT**.

Paint the backs of the petals with melted chocolate. Do not take the chocolate right to the edges of the petals. Allow to set at room temperature if possible. If not, a few seconds in the freezer will suffice.

When set, remove from mould and assemble the flower, using melted chocolate to secure the petals. Wipe the plastic moulds with tissue before re-using. **DO NOT WASH.**

A variety of chocolate decorations. The back row has chess pieces moulded from white chocolate; the roses have been made from coloured compounded chocolate and the front decorations are made from moulds and hand-coloured.

Chocolate Rose

Make five or six large rose petals. Make three or five small rose petals. Make three smaller petals for the centre.

Place a small daub of melted chocolate on to waxed paper. Arrange five or six large petals on the paper, overlapping them in a circle and when set add another small daub of melted chocolate and arrange three or five small petals inside the circle. Place three smaller petals into the centre of the rose in the same manner.

Bud

The bud is made in the same way as the centre of the rose.

Leaves

Brush chocolate on to the back of washed, fresh rose leaves. Allow to set and peel leaf off.

Chocolate Christmas Tree

Place the pattern on a board. Cover with waxed paper. Brush or pipe the chocolate on to the paper. Make six Christmas tree halves.

Join two pieces at the centre with chocolate, then add two more pieces standing them up in a V shape. When set, stand up and attach the last two pieces to the other side also in a V shape. Decorate with royal icing loops and coloured cachous.

These decorations are made from a variety of different chocolate recipes. The orchids are made from chocolate leather and the animals and eggs from moulded compounded chocolate.

These Christmas decorations are made by brushing chocolate on to the back of moulds cut from aluminium cans.

Chocolate Choir Boy and Angel

Angel

Cut the moulds and patterns from clean, undented aluminium drink cans. Be very careful of sharp edges.

Lower Skirt
Cut a 12 cm (5 in) circle, split to centre and wrap around twice to form a cone. Staple together.

Upper Skirt
Cut a 10 cm (4 in) circle and form a cone as above.

Sleeves and Wings
Cut two from pattern, curve slightly and cover with adhesive plastic. Leave a little extra around the edges.

Cut circles of Bake lining paper or waxed paper the same size as the upper and lower skirts. Cut to centre and roll to line the moulds.

Brush chocolate on to the paper and place the point of the mould into the neck of a jar to set. Remove cone and unwrap.

Brush chocolate on to the back of the patterns for sleeves and wings. Allow to set then peel off pattern. Make two buttons for the head.

Note: Bake lining paper may be used several times.

Choir Boy

Place the white upper skirt pattern (from the angel) over the milk chocolate lower skirt, using a daub of melted chocolate to secure.

Join white buttons for head and use a daub of melted chocolate on the skirt mould to secure.

Attach sleeves and head with a little melted chocolate and pipe the features on to the face. Use two blue sprinkles for the eyes. Pipe brown curly hair over the head. Pipe a white ruffle around the neck to cover the join.

Cocoa can be used to paint designs on cakes or plaques. On the right is a tiny floral plaque with a scalloped edge; below is a plaque with a Christmas touch finished with a piped border. (Isla Parkes, Zimbabwe)

Cocoa Painting

Cocoa painting has been practised by master chefs for centuries. It is done in monotone on a base of almond paste or marzipan, gum paste, moulding paste, sugar paste or rolled covering paste. The basis is similar to painting, and, like all areas in cake decorating, needs a lot of practice. Several water colour brushes are required—fine, medium and heavy. Suggested sizes are 4–6 round sable plus one flat firm brush. The materials used are powdered cocoa (dark continental brands give a wider range of tones) and cocoa butter which can be purchased from a pharmacist. As cocoa butter is very expensive, use Copha, Crisco or Holsum (solid white vegetable shortenings) as a substitute on your first attempt.

Superb earth tones can be obtained by using cocoa painting.

Step 1: Using the required medium, roll out a plaque about 1 cm (⅜ in) thick.

Step 2: Trace the selected pattern on to the prepared base, using a non-toxic pencil.

Step 3: Place a small quantity of cocoa butter into a container standing in warm water in an egg poacher or skillet. Keep it at a constant 37°C (98°F) temperature.

Step 4: Add a small quantity of sieved cocoa to the cocoa butter. Mix well. This is the basic light colour. Add a little more cocoa for a medium shade and still more cocoa for a darker shade.

Step 5: Paint the background first and move towards the front as in painting, filling in the foreground last.

Step 6: Highlights can be obtained by scraping with a craft knife, scalpel, cottonwool, toothpick or pin. Cocoa butter can also be used in conjunction with paste or powder colours and your picture may be painted in browns and highlighted in colour.

Keep your brushes as clean as possible and do not overload the brush. To get the effect of fur, use a stubby brush and avoid excessive detail. When dry, brush over with a soft brush to remove specks of cocoa. Highlight with lustre colour. Allow to dry in a cool place.

Cocoa painting gives a natural look to decorations.

Children's birthday cake with a rocket ship, space vehicles, flying saucers and satellites. (Margaret Tesorier)

Make Your Own Moulds

Knowing how to make your own favourite moulds is useful because it enables you to create all kinds of special decorations not available elsewhere. Even with the increasing availability of commercial moulds for cake decorating, often it is necessary to make your own. The methods described here are simple to master.

Delightful fun figures made from Pettinice or commercial rolled covering paste.

Method 1

Press a piece of moulding paste over the desired article. Carefully remove the paste and allow to set. You then have the negative mould from which to work.

Method 2

This method uses plaster of paris or dental plaster which is very fine and makes a good mould.

Place 500 g (1 lb) dental plaster or plaster of paris in a container with a little water. Mix to a thick creamy paste. Do not make it too runny. Thickly spread the paste onto an old flat surface, such as timber or plastic. Firmly press the lightly greased article into the plaster to take the impression. Leave to dry overnight. Carefully remove the impression and allow the cast to dry thoroughly before use. All types of moulds can be made, for example, dolls' heads, arms and legs, Wedgwood figures, baskets, etc.

Moulds can also be made from Fimo, Daz or putty, etc.

Rice Paper

Rice paper is a quick and easy way of decorating a children's cake with a favourite theme, and the paper is edible. It is also available in many colours and may be used as flat cut-outs, or for such things as a castle, a tree, an Indian tepee or a sailing boat, etc., that stand up on the cake. The design can be completed then placed on the cake with piping gel or icing, or, if the paper is already moist, it will adhere itself.

Rice paper is very brittle and easily broken, so it is advisable to gently roll the paper several times with a light rolling pin for easier handling.

Use liquid vegetable colouring sparingly on rice paper as the moisture will dissolve the paper. Draw or trace the design using a non-toxic fine point pen or paintbrush, non-toxic icing pen, non-toxic chalks and/or airbrush.

These decorations are made on rice paper with a piped edge in chocolate. The centres are filled with piping gel.

Step 1: Place the rice paper smooth side up over the design.

Step 2: Using a black fine-point non-toxic pencil, trace the entire design. Blot with blotting paper and leave to dry to prevent smudging when painting.

Step 3: Trim around the design with small scissors or a craft knife.

Step 4: Pipe the outline and details of the design in royal icing or piping chocolate (2–3 drops glycerine to 50 g compounded chocolate). Allow to dry.

Step 5: Colour small quantities of piping gel. Test the colour and consistency of gel on a spare piece of rice paper and if necessary thin with one or two drops of water. Do not add too much moisture to the paintbrush and apply colours sparingly.

Step 6: Paint one colour first in the various areas required being careful that colours do not bleed.

Step 7: If painting figures, add a little flesh colour to the face, neck, arms, hands and legs. Leave to dry. Work in advance and store in a cool place.

Rice paper may be placed on butter cream or rolled covering paste.

Hobby Dough

Flowers made using hobby dough last much longer than those made with royal icing. Spray with a clear lacquer for extra lasting quality.

Articles such as chunky necklets, earrings, floral plaques, bracelets and jewellery boxes may be moulded from hobby dough.

Note: Hobby dough is for display purposes only.

Australian wildflowers made from hobby dough in vivid colours. They are sprayed with clear lacquer for lasting quality.

1 cup (125 g/4 oz) cornflour (cornstarch)
1 cup (125 g/4 oz) plain (all-purpose) flour
1 cup (250 ml/8 fl oz) non-toxic all-purpose white liquid glue
1 tablespoon glycerine

Step 1: Place all the ingredients in a well-greased bowl. Beat well until the mixture sticks to the beaters.

Step 2: Remove the mixture from bowl and knead by hand until smooth (10–12 minutes). Add a little more glue if the mixture is too dry. Store in an airtight container.

COURTESY FRANCES KUYPER, LOS ANGELES, USA

Teapot made with Pettinice frills and a frangipani spray. (Carol Axford)

Airbrushing, Cake Crafting and Figure Piping

Airbrushing, cake crafting and figure piping are all specialties of Frances Kuyper. Frances is a well-known American cake decorator. Based in Los Angeles, she travels extensively as a demonstrator and promoter of cake decorating.

Airbrushed baby portrait on a gum paste plaque.

Airbrushing a Baby Portrait

Portraits should not be attempted until you are proficient at basic airbrush techniques. Once you have learned to control the airbrush, you will be able to do any photo or pattern. Blending colours is important.

To apply dark colours, hold the air brush about 2.5 cm (1 in) above the surface. For a lot of colour pull well back on the trigger.

For a fine line release the trigger slightly. For a heavy line pull back the trigger. Move the airbrush in and out from the surface until you feel comfortable with the process.

Prepare the gum paste plaque and make sure it is thoroughly dry before working on it. Trace the pattern on to white paper. Lay the paper face down on the plaque and scribble over the back with a soft lead pencil. Try not to hold the paper where pattern lines are, as this may cause smudges. The pattern lines should be just visible on the plaque.

Prepare your airbrush for spraying. Commence with brown shadows, then flesh tones. For yellow hair, use a drop of brown colour with yellow in the colour cup. Place your thumb over the cup and shake to mix. Use pink for cheeks, holding the air brush far away for the blush in the cheeks. Also, fill in the lips with pink. Do not outline the lips with brown or black. Outline the eyes and eye lashes and also the iris with black. Fill in the pupil of the eye, leaving the highlight white. Hold the airbrush far away again and fill the background with the desired colour.

The plaque may be applied to a cake. Cut a piece of waxed paper about 1.25 cm (½ in) smaller than the plaque. Place on the cake and attach with royal icing. Place the plaque on the waxed paper. It can be removed and kept as a keepsake.

Cake Crafting

Cake crafting is a quick and easy method of decorating a cake by embossing and lifting decorations onto the covering rather than adding them later.

Cover the cake with rolled covering paste; if you wish a bevel edge place a roll of fondant around the base of the cake before covering. Use a small scoop to slant and smooth the bevel.

As soon as the cake is covered, make the desired impressions in the cake covering using crimpers or special cake crafting tools. Many items in the kitchen can be used as embossing tools.

Trace a pattern on the cake top as described above. Emboss the design by cutting into the icing with a bent tapered spatula. Follow the pattern from the centre and work outwards. Skim very carefully under the design parts and lift and shape as you desire. Colour with an airbrush.

Figure Piping

Figures and shapes to decorate novelty cakes can be created simply and easily by piping over a cake base. Cup cakes can be used to build up the shape quickly. The figures can be piped in coloured icing or airbrushed later. Any soft icing can be used.

Clown

Using No. 32 tip and heavy pressure, pull upward and make a large mound for the body. Draw out the legs in front of the body. Start at the shoulder and make a semi-circle on either side for the arms. With yellow icing and No. 67 tip, hold the tip upright and use heavy pressure to make ruffles around the neck, arms and legs. Insert a straw through the centre of the body with the end protruding.

Insert No. 10 tip over the straw and using heavy pressure, raise the tube to form the head. Using a small tube of red icing, squiggle the hair then make a red nose, eyebrows and mouth. Use black for the eyes and orange for the hands which are formed by making a ball of icing and inserting the tip into the ball to shape the fingers. Use white for the shoes and start at base. Begin with heavy pressure, then light then heavy again.

Christmas Tree

Place an ice cream cone upside down on the cake. Using green icing and No. 67 leaf tip, start at top point of tree. Hold the tip straight and make a figure eight, increasing the width of the stroke to the base. Continue in this manner around the cone. Sprinkle with caster (powdered) sugar over the tree to resemble snow.

Lion

You will need a cup cake for the head. Place the cup cake on its side two-thirds off centre of the cake top. The top of the cup cake will be the face. Make two strokes in front of the cup cake for paws. With a No. 10 tip and beige coloured icing, use hard pressure and start from the back of the cup cake. Swing away about 5 cm (2 in) narrowing a little. Lift the tip and squeeze harder to make a mound. Push down on the tip, squeezing lightly, then lift again, squeezing harder to make the haunch. Continue releasing the pressure making a comma stroke.

Pipe a straight line for the leg. Pipe three very tiny strokes to make his knuckles. Using a No. 6 tip and light

Opposite above: *Novelty figures can be piped on to a cake base for a quick and easy decoration.*

Opposite below: *Rather than add a decoration to a cake after covering, you can lift a design out of the covering itself. This is a simple method requiring only a few minutes of time.*

Any figure can be piped using the basic shapes outlined in the pattern section.

pressure pipe the tail. Make a thick stroke on the top front of the cup cake, for the forehead. Just below each end of the forehead on the outside of the cup cake make two balls of icing for the ears. Make a ball of icing for each cheek. Starting from chin position and using a flat stroke move upward to reach the forehead. Use a little harder pressure and pull out to make the snout. With No. 7 tip and brown icing, pipe a few tassels over the forehead and the end of the tail. Rough up this icing to make it look like a mane.

Cut a tiny hole in a piping bag and using black icing, outline the edge of the mouth and place dots for the eyes. Cut a tiny V in a very small bag of red icing. Holding the bag flat, commence from the inside of the mouth and pull out the tongue. Cut a small hole in the tip and pipe three teeth on either side of the top and bottom of the mouth.

Tree Stump

Use two cup cakes top to top and insert a straw for support. Using No. 32 tip make a spiral pinwheel on top, smoothing with a small bent spatula. Start at the base and with upward strokes cover the cup cakes completely. Draw out a few strands at different intervals around the base for roots. Use the tip of a bent spatula to rough the surface to resemble bark.

Hold the airbrush a few centimetres away and spray the entire sides dark brown. Use a light colour for the top, making a spiral pinwheel for the age marks. Hold the airbrush sideways to hit the side of the stump with black to give a realistic bark effect.

Pink Elephant

Using No. 10 tip and pink icing, pipe a very large pear shape for the body. Make a ball of icing for the head at the narrow end of the pear, lift the tube and then decrease pressure pulling out the trunk in a downward motion. Insert the tip into the body at the shoulder area and pull out two stumps for the front legs. To make the back legs insert the tube into the side of the base and using heavy pressure, move the tube upwards and pull towards you. Stop the pressure and run the tip of the tube to make a smooth edge.

Using a small cut tip on a tube of white icing, insert on either side of the trunk and pull out the tusks. Insert No. 124 rose tube on each side of the head and pull up and out to form large ears. Use the small white tube to make toe nails. Use a small tube of red icing to make red crosses for the eyes.

Note: This shape can be used as the base for the other figure illustrated.

Dog Face

Start at the toe area and pipe a shape resembling a shell. Decrease the pressure slightly, then move the tube upward. Using brown or black icing and No. 2 tube use heavy pressure to make the ears. Add little black dots for the eyes and two little curved lines for the mouth.

Note: This shape can be used as the base for the other figures illustrated.

Father Christmas plaque made by piping directly onto the base and airbrushing on the colour.

Clothesline

Using black icing with No. 1 tip, make a line across the cake. With No. 104 rose tip, place the thin part against the line and make a curve to form a diaper. Add as many diapers as required. Using yellow icing and No. 1 tip, make an up-and-down motion on the corners of each diaper to form clothes pegs. Use No. 1 tip to print a letter on each diaper.

Swan

Using any size tip, make a curve resembling a question mark. As you get to the base, increase the pressure. Make a large egg shape for the body. Using No. 6 tip, pull out small strokes for the wings. Using No. 2 tip, make two curved strokes for the bill. Add a little stroke of black next to the bill and then add a black eye.
Note: This shape can be used as the base for the other figures illustrated.

Father Christmas

Father Christmas can be made in any size by changing the tips. Use flesh coloured icing and make a hot dog shape. Make two balls of icing on either side for the cheeks. Make a small ball in the centre for the nose. Use No. 10 tip with red icing and make a shell shape for the mouth giving it a little curve. Pipe a curve in red icing for the hat.

With a star tip, start at the right side of the face and pipe the beard by making a zigzag and increasing the length of the stroke towards the centre of the chin. Decrease again as you travel up the left side. Make a zigzag for the fur on the hat. Make a pompom and a handlebar moustache. Pipe little curves for the eye brows. Use black icing to pipe the eyes.

Comparison of Australian, U. K. and American Piping Tubes

Australian	U. K.	American
7 mm	No. 4	No. 10 large writing tube
4 mm	No. 3	No. 7 large writing tube
3 mm	No. 2	No. 6 large writing tube
star No. 15	No. 15	32 large star tube
No. 17	medium leaf tube	67 leaf tube
No. 20 L	No. 59	124 large petal tube
No. 1	No. 1	2 writing tube
No. 0	No. 0	1 writing tube

Above: *Special occasion cake with azaleas, embossed cupids and edge finished with petal dust.*

Opposite: *Three-tiered oval wedding cake with each tier swivelled slightly to increase interest. Each tier has double extension work, flowers under the bridge and a spray of orchids on top.* (Dorothy Moore)

Cake Sculpture

Cake sculpture is fun. If you enjoyed sticky hands and making mud pies then you will enjoy this creative area of cake decorating. If you do not have the flair for freehand modelling do not despair, there are a few basic rules which will enable anyone to do a cake sculpture.

After you have decided on the subject and the desired size, proportion needs to be determined. The easiest way to achieve this is to select a suitable model—a child's toy or picture. Toys are the best to use as they give a three-dimensional shape to copy when sculpting. It is sometimes difficult to imagine what the features should be like when using a flat picture.

The next step is to produce a drawing of your design so that you can blow it up to the required size. If you are using a toy, trace a basic outline by lying it flat on a piece of paper and drawing around it. The drawing may be increased in size by using a photocopier or a grid drawn over the small drawing to use as a base.

The enlarged drawing will give you measurements to work to, determining the amount and shape of cakes that will be needed to complete the sculpture.

If the chosen subject is to be flat on the board, then the enlarged drawing may be used as an outline to cut the external shape before modelling the upper features.

Try to keep the external features simple. For example arms should be close to the body, not extended. If the shape of the model is elongated or thin, it is easier to have it lying flat. I have given instructions for a teddy bear. I hope you have as much fun as I did.

Opposite: *Friendly bear is sculpted from cake and then covered.* (Lyne Fuller)

Teddy Bear

Requirements:

	Small Bear	Large Bear	
Body	2 x 15 cm (6 in)	2 x 25 cm (10 in)	round
Head	1 x 10 cm (4 in)	1 x 20 cm (8 in)	round
Legs	1 x 15 cm (6 in)	1 x 20 cm (8 in)	square
For shaping	1 x 250 g (8 oz)	1 x 500 g (1 lb)	cake mixed with jam (preferably apricot)
Covering	1.75 kg (4 lb)	3.5 kg (8 lb)	rolled covering paste coloured brown or cream
Board	37 cm dia. x 12 mm (15 in dia. x ½ in)	75 cm dia. x 12 mm (30 in dia. x ½ in)	chip board
Supports	45 cm x 50 mm (18 x ¼ in)	1 metre x 50 mm (36 x ½ in)	dowel
	1 plastic fork	1 plastic fork	
	6 small pieces 50 mm (¼ in)	6 small pieces 50 mm (¼ in)	dowel

Shaping

Body: Place the two large round cakes for the body on the board. Secure with jam between the cakes and on the board. Round the edges and cut a little out of the front of the cake where the legs will be positioned. Trim the bottom edge so that it curves under.

Legs: Cut the square leg cake in half. Cut off the corners on the long side and cut the ends to fit into the body. Place a mound of cake and jam mixture on the end of the leg and mould into a foot shape. Use extra cake mix to shape the leg. Smooth down.

Head: Cut a 5 cm (2 in) piece from the round head cake and place on the body, cut side down, towards the back. Push the long dowel through the head and body down to the board to support the head. Cut off the dowel close to the cake.

Using the cake and jam mixture, shape the face on the front of the head. Before completing the features, push the plastic fork through the thickest parts to help support the face. Shape the snout, eyes and ears. Make the ears short for ease of covering.

Finish shaping the bear with the cake and jam mixture. The arms are attached later for ease of covering.

Covering

It is easier to cover the bear in sections because the fur pattern must be applied to the surface fairly quickly. After covering each section, mark the vertical lines of the fur pattern with a fork and then use scissors to cut lines at random to give the fur effect. Ensure that the scissor cuts are small and always in the same direction. Use a large soft brush to remove the excess covering.

Body: The body is covered in two parts. Join the icing at each side so that the seam will be covered by the arms. Rub the join together and make sure that the fur marking conceals the join. Press well into the neck area. Pay particular attention to the leg seam to blend successfully.

Legs: Cover each leg separately and shape the sole of each foot and toes with a modelling tool. Don't forget to form claws!

Head: Cover the head in one piece, taking care to retain the shape of the face and ears. Mark the eyes, nose and mouth before marking the fur. Remember to leave the inside of the ear smooth.

Arms: Mould the arms from rolled covering paste and attach with water. Support the arms until set and secure with a small piece of dowel. It is best to attach the arms after the body covering has set (approximately 24 hours). This prevents accidental flattening of the fur.

Finishing Touches

Paint the pupils of eyes then the nose and mouth. Mix the colour with alcohol and spray over the fur. (Water softens the icing and takes a long time to dry.) An airbrush is ideal, but I successfully used a small spray bottle. A brush tends to smooth the fur and the result is not as effective.

Set the bear on a bed of green coconut around the base on thinned royal icing. Tie a ribbon around the neck.

This may sound like a lot of hard work and it is! But it's also a lot of fun.

COURTESY LYNE FULLER, SYDNEY, AUSTRALIA

Opposite: *Anniversary cake with frilled base topped with ribbon, silver inscription and waterlily spray.*

Recipes

Royal Icing

Royal icing is for piping. It should be made carefully, so take the time to mix it well. Buy your pure icing sugar from a busy supermarket to ensure its freshness and squeeze or shake the box before purchasing as a double check. Allow the egg to come to room temperature before using, then separate the white, making sure none of the yolk is included. Be sure all utensils are free from all grease, as this can ruin the icing.

1 egg white
¼ teaspoon liquid glucose (optional)
1½ cups (250 g/8 oz) pure icing (confectioners) sugar
2 or 3 drops acetic acid

Beat the egg white and liquid glucose lightly in a glass bowl with a wooden spoon. Add the finely sieved icing sugar, one tablespoon at a time, beating well after each addition. Beat until the mixture is thick and creamy. Add the acetic acid and beat until blended. The icing should form and hold a smooth peak when pulled away from the mixture. (Beating time is approximately 20 minutes.) Keep in an airtight container, or cover with a damp cloth or plastic film to prevent crusting.

Actiwhite Royal Icing

3 teaspoons actiwhite powder or egg albumen
4 tablespoons water
3 cups (500 g/1 lb) pure icing (confectioners) sugar

Actiwhite powder is available from healthfood stores. Soak the powder in water for 15 minutes and sieve through muslin or a fine sieve. Add the icing sugar slowly and beat for 6 minutes at full speed, 15 minutes at half speed, until the mixture becomes very thick. Store in a refrigerator and re-beat before use. Use water to correct the consistency. Before use, work the air bubbles out of the royal icing and beat it until it is shiny and smooth.

Draw a pencil line and run a small quantity of icing over the line—if it covers the line, it is ready for use.

For large areas, have several plastic sandwich bags filled with the icing and snip the corner just before commencing to flood.

Moulding Paste

Moulding paste is used for moulded flowers, leaves, ornaments, Christmas decorations, wedding bells, bowls, etc. Follow the recipe carefully as correct consistency is of prime importance, especially for fine petals.

6 teaspoons (1 fl oz) cold water
2 teaspoons gelatine
1 teaspoon liquid glucose
1 cup (300 g/5 oz) pure icing (confectioners) sugar
extra sifted icing (confectioners) sugar for kneading

Place the water in a double saucepan, add the gelatine and stir over low heat until dissolved. ***(Do not boil.)*** Add the glucose and stir until dissolved. Allow to cool, but not to become cold. Add the icing sugar, stirring until it is absorbed. Place in an airtight container and leave for 24 hours. The mixture should be firm and spongy when set.

When ready to commence moulding, take a small quantity of the mixture and knead in the extra sifted icing sugar until it is of a similar consistency to plasticine. Moulding fondant keeps for longer periods if this method is used.

Rolled Buttercream

250 g (8 oz) butter
1 cup light Karo syrup
1 teaspoon vanilla essence
½ teaspoon salt
3 cups (1 kg/2 lb) pure icing (confectioners) sugar, approximately

Place the butter in a bowl and stir until creamy. Add the syrup and continue stirring until mixed. Add the icing sugar gradually until the mixture thickens. Transfer the mixture on to board and knead in more sugar until the mixture thickens like toffee–depending on the weather. Knead until the icing becomes very smooth.

When ready for use the mixture should not stick to your hands. Rolled buttercream will keep for months if refrigerated in a tightly sealed container. Bring to room temperature before using.

To cover cake
Place a heavy crumb coat on the cake, with a minimum of filling between the layers. Roll out icing between two sheets of heavy plastic film to the desired size and shape. Peel the top piece of plastic off, turn it over and place on cake, peel the second piece off gently and smooth icing using a hot spatula.

Moulding
Add enough icing sugar to make a very firm consistency then use this to mould simple shapes such as fruits, animals, etc. Dust the mould lightly first with cornflour (cornstarch). If the mixture is soft, place it in the refrigerator to firm, then mould.

Pouring Fondant

3 cups (500 g/1 lb) pure icing (confectioners) sugar
6 tablespoons hot water
food colouring
1 tablespoon liquid glucose

Sieve the sugar and place in a bowl with a lip. Add the hot water, 2 tablespoons at a time stirring constantly with a wooden spoon. Beat well after each addition. When the fondant coats the back of a spoon add the colour and glucose. Mix well. If the mixture is too thick add 1 teaspoon of water. Use as required.

Net Stiffener

Cotton net needs to be stiffened so that it will retain the desired shape for the decoration. This mixture gives good results. If stored in the refrigerator, the mixture will keep for several months.

¾ (250 g/4 oz) pure icing (confectioners) sugar
½ cup (125 ml/4 fl oz) cold water

Dissolve the icing sugar in the cold water and bring it slowly to the boil. Simmer gently for 10 minutes, cool and bottle.

Marzipan

This marzipan recipe is recommended for moulding figures. You can develop your own ideas for moulded decorations with a little practice.

⅓ cup (250 g/8 oz) liquid glucose
1.5 kg (3 lb) prepared commercial marzipan
6 cups (1 kg/2 lb) pure icing (confectioners) sugar

Soften the glucose over hot water using a double saucepan. Blend with the marzipan, stirring to a smooth paste. Add the icing sugar gradually, kneading until the dough is firm and pliable. Colour as desired.

Opposite: *Birthday cake with dartboard and darts, side embroidery and silver ribbon trim.* (Carol Axford)

Stephen

Flower Paste

Used worldwide, this recipe is particularly suitable for making fine petals, cut from the thinly rolled paste.

3 cups (500 g/1 lb) pure icing (confectioners) sugar
3 teaspoons gum tragacanth
2 teaspoons gelatine
5 teaspoons cold water
2 teaspoons Copha or solid white vegetable shortening
2 teaspoons liquid glucose

Lightly grease two basins with extra Copha. Place half the icing sugar in each basin. Add the gum tragacanth to the sugar in one basin; cover with a clean dry tea-towel and a plate, and place over boiling water in a saucepan. Heat over low heat until the sugar is hot to the touch.

Meanwhile, place the cold water in a small metal container and sprinkle the gelatine over the surface. Let stand until the gelatine becomes spongy. Dissolve over hot (*not boiling*) water until it becomes completely clear. Stir occasionally to prevent a skin from forming. When the gelatine is clear, add the Copha and the liquid glucose and dissolve these too.

Add the dissolved gelatine mixture and the egg white to the sugar in the bowl on the stove. Keep the basin over the hot water on the stove and use a metal spoon. Add quickly before stirring, then stir briskly until the mixture turns from a beige to a good white. This takes quite a long time. Make sure that the saucepan does not boil dry. When this mixture is quite white, add it to the sugar in the second basin, stirring until it becomes too stiff to stir easily. Dispense with the spoon. Wash, dry and lightly grease hands, and knead until all the sugar is incorporated. Pull the paste as for toffee, until it is very white and pliable. Place in a clean plastic bag in an airtight container in the fridge. Store for 24 hours before use.

COURTESY DENISE FRYER AND TOMBI PECK

Gum Paste

Gum paste is used for single shapes that can be modelled quickly, e.g., small animals on a log cake. It is not recommended for flowers.

3 cups (500 g/1 lb) pure icing (confectioners) sugar
2 teaspoons gelatine
¼ cup (65 ml/2 fl oz) boiling water

Sift the icing sugar. Thoroughly dissolve the gelatine in boiling water and add to half the quantity of icing sugar in a large bowl. Knead well, adding more icing sugar until the mixture is no longer sticky. Keep in a plastic bag in an airtight container

Pastillage

Pastillage, a mixture of royal icing and gum tragacanth, is used for modelling where strength is required, for instance, for houses, churches, etc. Pastillage sets firmly in most weather. Chemists stock gum tragacanth, however it may have to be ordered in advance. Sprinkle half a teaspoon of gum tragacanth into a cup of well-worked royal icing and beat thoroughly with a knife. Place in an airtight container, allow to stand for 24 hours. Take desired quantity from the container, and add enough pure icing sugar to form a pliable dough (like plasticine). Knead well. Do not store in the refrigerator. Store in a plastic bag in an airtight container.

Boiled Almond Paste

This is a rich almond paste, used only on very special cakes. A confectionery thermometer is used in this recipe.

4 cups (1 kg/2 lb) crystal sugar
½ cup (150 g/5 oz) glucose
1 cup (250 ml/8 fl oz) water
6¾ cups (750 g/1½ lb) ground almonds
4 tablespoons rum
1 egg
4 egg yolks
6 cups (1 kg/2 lb) pure icing (confectioners) sugar, sifted

Combine the sugar, glucose and water in a saucepan and stir until the sugar dissolves. Add a confectionery thermometer, then boil to 110°C (235°F). Allow to cool slightly, then add the ground almonds, rum, egg and egg yolks. Mix well and add the icing sugar, kneading well.

Toffee Glaze for Marzipan Fruit

This glaze can become sticky and soft in very humid weather, so it's best to apply coating the day it is required.

¼ cup (65 ml/2 fl oz) water
½ cup (125 g/4 oz) crystal sugar
pinch of cream of tartar

Grease a cake cooler to place the glazed fruit. Place the ingredients in a saucepan and stir gently over moderate heat until the sugar has dissolved. Increase the heat and boil rapidly (without stirring) until the mixture changes to light golden. Remove the glaze from the heat, place fruit one at a time on a fine-pronged fork and dip quickly into the glaze to obtain a thin coating. Place on the cooler to set.

Above: *Special occasion cake with extension work, lace, satin ribbon and four perfect magnolias.* (Norma Farrell)
Below: *Birthday cake with shaded frill to match the dog roses in the top spray and brush embroidery roses on the side.*

Butter Icing

125 g (4 oz) butter
1½ cups (250 g/8 oz) pure icing (confectioners) sugar, sifted
2 tablespoons sherry, lemon or orange juice

Cream the butter and icing sugar, add the liquid and beat until smooth. Spread evenly over the cake with a knife that has been dipped in milk.

Vienna Icing

Add 2 tablespoons sifted cocoa to the butter icing to make Vienna icing.

Supreme Covering Paste

A confectionery thermometer is required to make this excellent covering. Make it at least one week before it is required.

Group A
⅔ cup (150 ml/5 fl oz) water
⅓ cup (125 g/4 oz) liquid glucose
2 cups (500 g/1 lb) crystal sugar
1 teaspoon (30 ml/1 fl oz) glycerine
1 teaspoon cream of tartar

Group B
30 g (1 oz) gelatine
⅔ cup (150 ml/5 fl oz) water
125 g (4 oz) Copha or other solid white vegetable shortening
13½ cups (2.25 kg/4½ lb) pure icing (confectioners) sugar, sifted

Boil Group A to 120°C (240°F) or to soft-ball consistency when tested in cold water. Remove from heat and allow bubbles to subside. From Group B, dissolve the gelatine in the water, and add to mixture. Add the chopped Copha and allow to cool. Beat in half the icing sugar gradually. Place in a sealed plastic container and leave for at least 1 week, or until required. Before using, knead in the balance of the sifted icing sugar until a plastic consistency is obtained. This mixture will cover a large two tier cake, a small three tier cake, or three single 250 g (8 oz) cakes.

Applying Covering Paste

Clean the surface on which you are to work, and dust it with pure icing sugar. Place the paste on the surface and use a long rolling pin that has been lightly dusted with pure icing sugar. Roll it out to about 10 mm (⅜ in) thick and large enough to cover the top and sides of the cake. Brush the cake lightly with beaten egg white; drape the paste over a rolling pin, then lift carefully on to the cake, making sure it is evenly distributed. Care must be taken not to stretch the paste. Dust the palms of your hands with pure icing sugar. Smooth the top of the cake first to eliminate air bubbles; cupping your hand, work the corners. Use the palms of your hands to smooth the sides. With a knife held vertically, trim the paste into the base. Take care not to cut the paste too short (patching is always visible).

Moulding Paste

500 g (1 lb) Pettinice or commercial moulding paste
½ teaspoon egg white or 1 teaspoon egg powder
1 teaspoon gum tragacanth
½ teaspoon Copha or solid white shortening

Paint over the Pettinice with the egg white. Sprinkle the gum tragacanth into the mixture. Grease hands with ½ teaspoon Copha and knead the mixture well. Allow to stand overnight before use.

Marble Cake

This cake is used mainly for Dolly Varden cakes, its colours being one of the main attractions. A specially shaped Dolly Varden tin is used. This quantity fits into the standard sized tin.

250 g (8 oz) butter
1 cup (250 g/8 oz) crystal sugar
3 eggs
⅓ cup (75 ml/2½ fl oz) milk
vanilla essence
3 cups (360 g/12 oz) self-raising flour
few drops red colouring
2 tablespoons sifted cocoa

Grease and line the tin. Cream the butter and sugar, add well-beaten eggs, mixing well. Add the milk and vanilla, then the sifted flour. Divide the mixture in three equal parts; leave one part plain; add red colouring to the next; and add cocoa to the third. Place alternate spoonfuls in the tin. Bake in a moderate oven for 1 hour.

Large Rich Butter Cake

This mixture will fill a 23 cm (9 in) square tin, 8 cm (3 in) deep. This cake is firm enough to hold a thin coating of marzipan and covering paste.

375 g (12 oz) butter
2 cups (420 g/14 oz) caster (powdered) sugar
2 teaspoons vanilla essence
7 eggs
6 cups (750 g/1½ lb) self-raising flour
1 cup (250 ml/8 fl oz) milk, approximately

Cream the butter and sugar then add the vanilla. Add the eggs one at a time beating well after each addition. Add the milk and flour alternately in small quantities, mixing thoroughly. Pour into a well-greased tin. Bake in a moderate oven 180°C (350°/Gas 4) for 1½ hours, until golden brown on top. Cool in the tin.

Genoise Cake

This recipe is suitable for making *petits fours*, or fancy shapes. If possible, allow cake to stand for about 24 hours before cutting or place in freezer for a short time, then it will cut without crumbling.

½ cup (60 g/2 oz) self-raising flour
1 tablespoon cornflour (cornstarch)
3 eggs
½ cup (125 g/4 oz) crystal sugar
90 g (3 oz) butter or margarine, melted

Sift the flour and cornflour. Place the eggs and sugar in a basin over warm water and whisk lightly until the mixture is stiff enough to retain the impression of the whisk for a few seconds. Remove the basin from heat. Sift half the flour mixture over the surface and fold in *very lightly*. Add the balance of the flour in the same way, followed by the melted butter. Pour into a greased and lined slab tin and bake in a moderate oven until golden brown (about 45 minutes depending on depth of tin).

Children's party cakes made from the genoise mixture may be baked in ice cream cones and decorated with hundreds and thousands, jelly beans or other small sweets.

Oblong birthday cake with double fuchsia spray, side embroidery and scalloped frill.

Rich Fruit Cake

This quantity makes one 20 cm (8 in) square or one 22 cm (9 in) round cake.

1⅔ cups (250 g/8 oz) currants
1½ cups (250 g/8 oz) sultanas
1½ cups (250 g/8 oz) raisins
½ cup (90 g/3 oz) dates
½ cup (90 g/3 oz) prunes
⅓ cup (60 g/2 oz) mixed peel
⅓ cup (60 g/ 2 oz) glacé cherries
½ cup (60 g/2 oz) dried apricots
½ cup (60 g/2 oz) dried pineapple
⅓ cup (60 g/2 oz) chopped glacé figs, optional
⅓ cup (60 g/2 oz) chopped glacé ginger, optional
½ cup (60 g/2 oz) slivered almonds
250 g (8 oz) butter
1½ cups (250 g/8 oz) moist brown sugar or black if available
5 medium eggs
1 tablespoon plum jam
1 teaspoon vanilla essence
1 teaspoon Parisienne essence
2 teaspoons molasses, golden syrup or treacle
1 teaspoon glycerine
juice of 1 medium lemon
1 teaspoon almond essence, optional
2¼ cups (300 g/10 oz) plain (all-purpose) flour
1 teaspoon ground nutmeg
1 teaspoon ground cinnamon
1 teaspoon ground mixed spice
2 tablespoons sherry or rum

Cut the fruit into small uniform pieces and soak, with the almonds, in 2 tablespoons each of sherry, rum and brandy for at least 24 hours. The longer you leave it, the better the flavour. Stir daily to evenly distribute the alcohol through the fruit.

Cream the butter and sugar then add the eggs one at a time. Beat only until you have a smooth batter. Do not overbeat. Gradually add the fluid to the batter mixing very carefully.

Sift the flour and spices and add alternately with the fruit.

Use your hand to thoroughly mix the fruit and flour into the batter.

Pour into a lined cake tin and place on a low shelf in a cold oven. Turn oven to 140°C (275°F/Gas 1) for approximately 3½ hours. While hot pour over the sherry or rum. Allow to cool in the tin.

Note: Mixture may be made and stored in the freezer for up to 6 months before cooking. Bring to room temperature and place in the tin. Cook in usual way.

Above: *Two-tiered wedding cake on unusual stand with pink roses arranged with blue ribbon to match the frilled base.*

Opposite: *Unusual two-tiered wedding cake in black and white on a perspex stand. The extension work has been coloured to match the floral spray.*

Two-tiered wedding cake with Australian waratahs on perspex stand.

Two-tiered wedding cake with scalloped extension work, side embroidery and a spray of strelitzia, tiger lilies and baby's breath on each tier.

Step-by-Step

Above: *Edge made with ejection cutter flowers after extension work was dry. The edge is dusted with petal dust to match the flowers.*

Below: *Cutter pieces can be used in place of a piped bridge.*

Examples of brush embroidery used for side decorations.

Above and opposite: *Quick and simple piped side designs. Measure accurately.*

Above and opposite: *Various embroidery designs.*

Coloured Pettinice designs for use on the edges of cakes.

Patterns

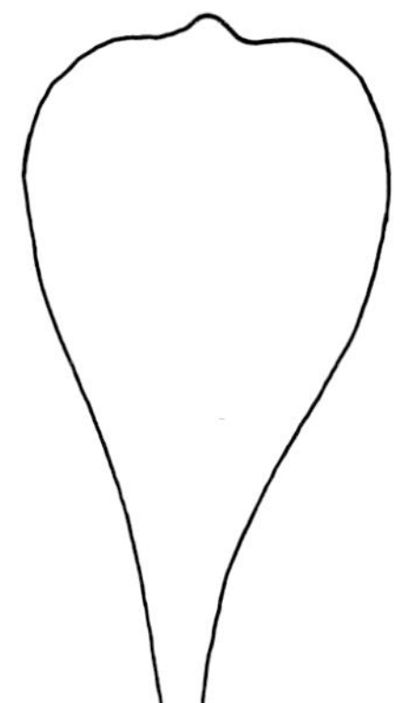
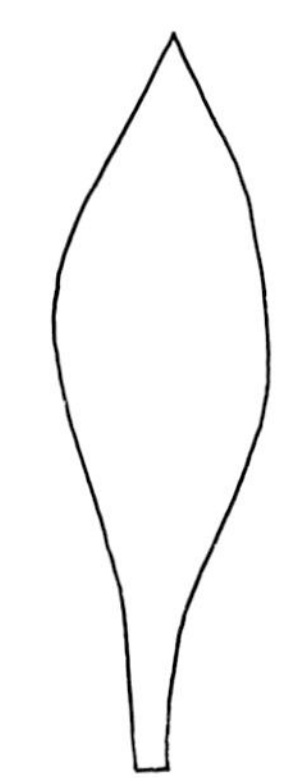

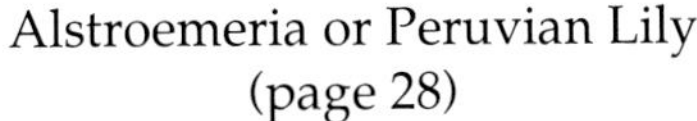

Alstroemeria or Peruvian Lily
(page 28)

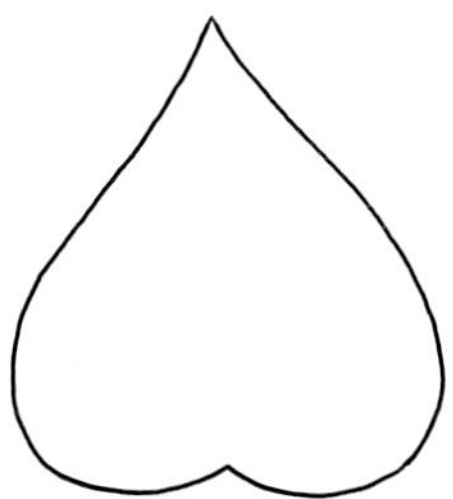

Bougainvillea
(page 26)

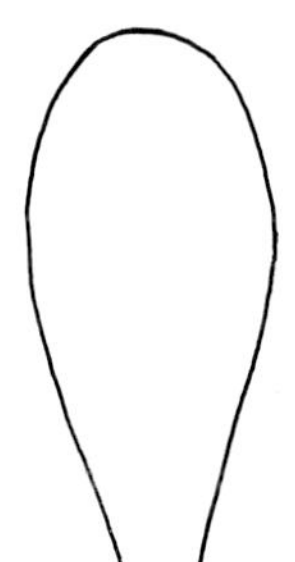

Wild Iris
(page 33)

Rose

Dwarf Azaleas
(page 20)

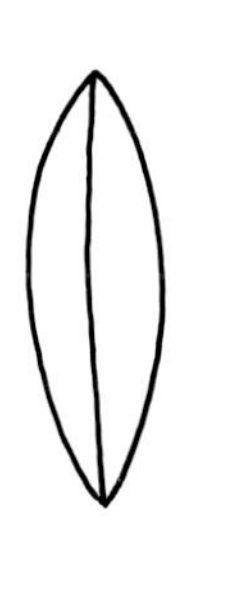
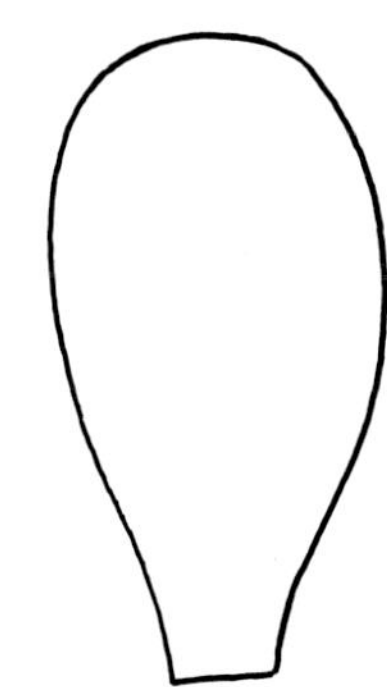

Azaleas
(page 25)

Wedding Bells
(page 23)

Blue Butterfly Bush
(page 25)

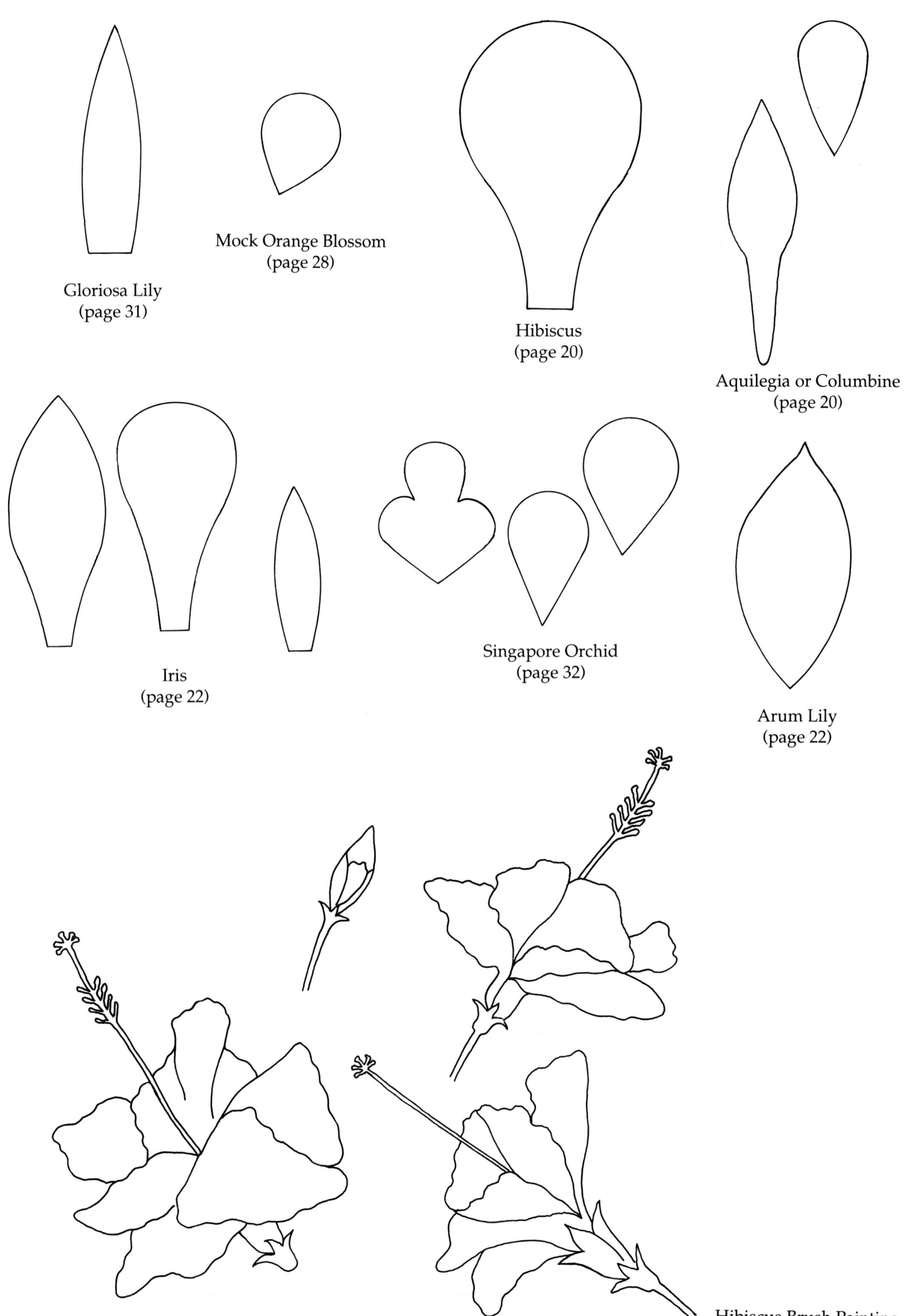

Hibiscus Brush Painting

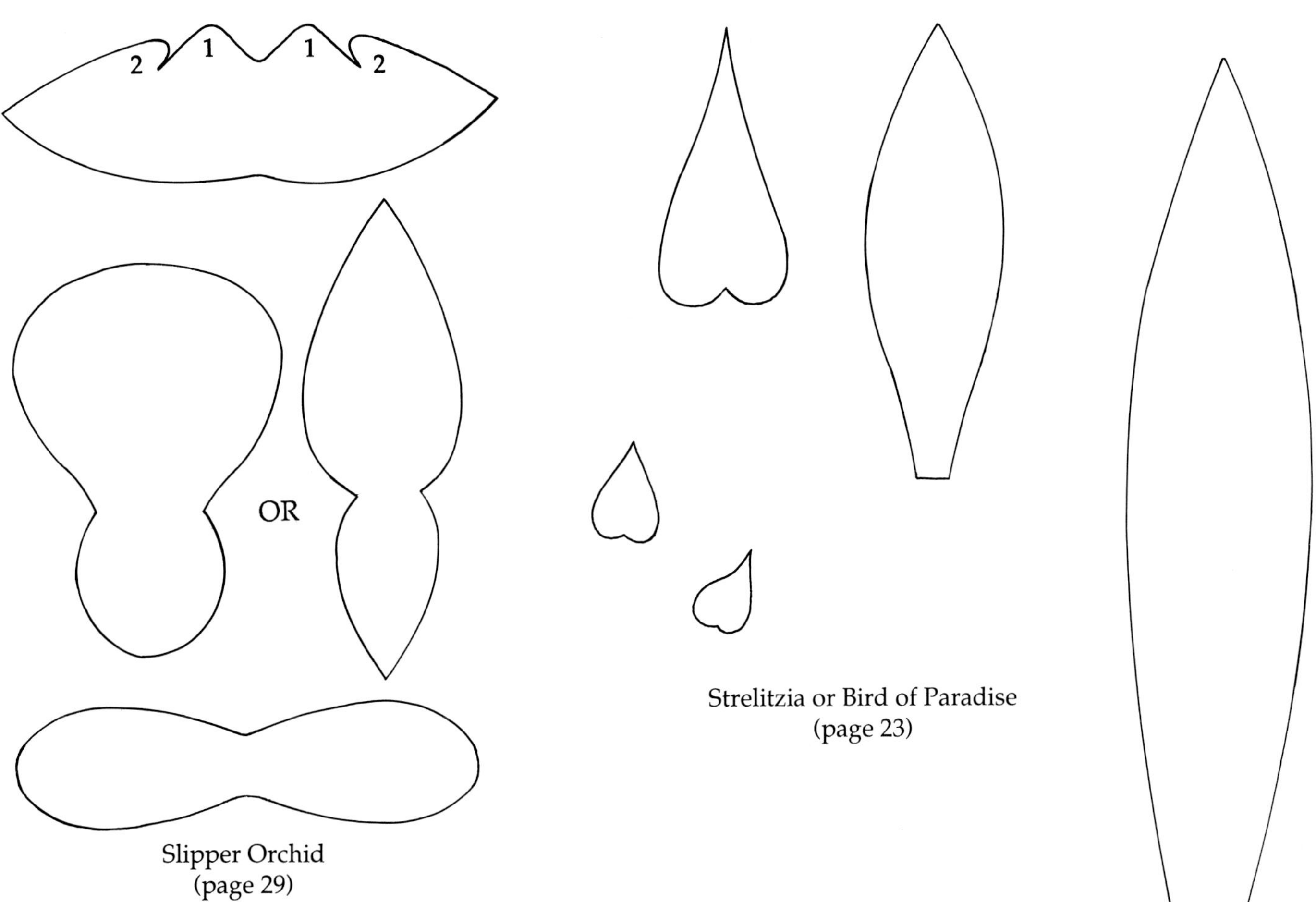

Slipper Orchid
(page 29)

Strelitzia or Bird of Paradise
(page 23)

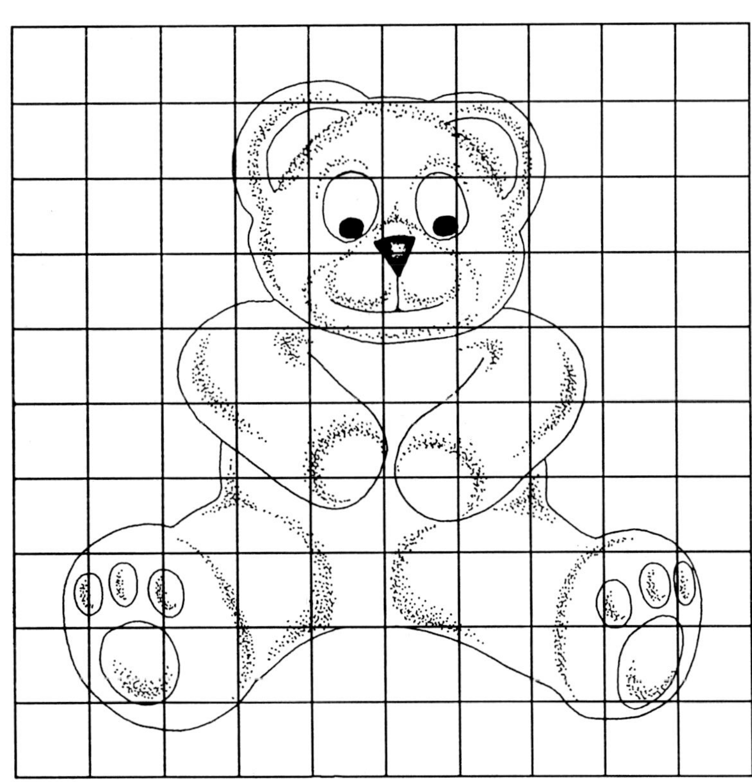

Teddy Bear
(page 70)

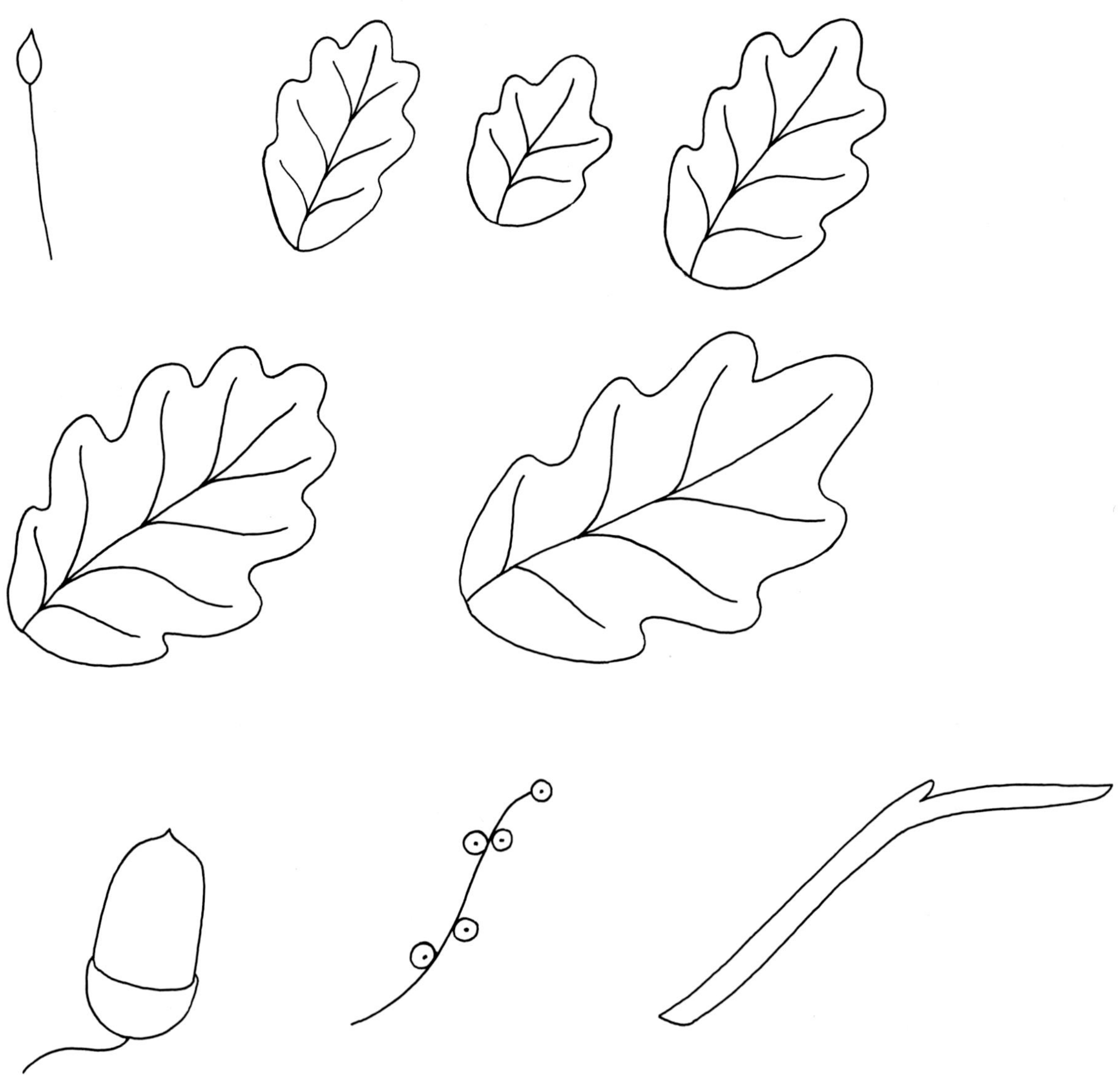

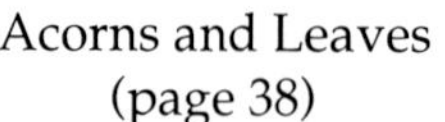

Acorns and Leaves
(page 38)

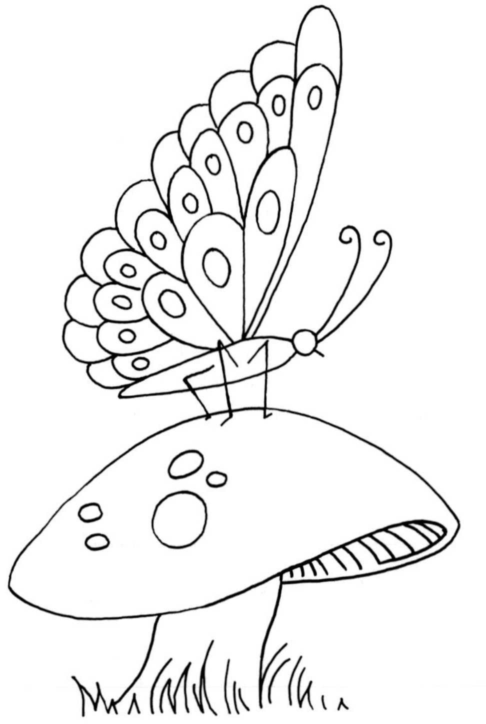

Shell border

Drop loops using No. 0 tube in the same colour as cake.
Bows and dots using No. 0 tube and contrasting colour.

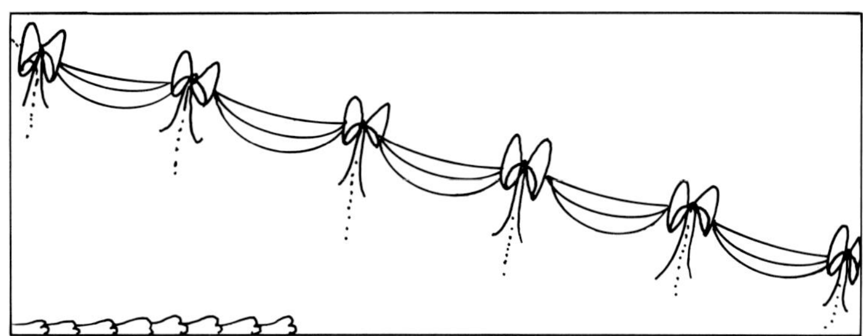

Shell border

Loops and dots using No. 0 tube.

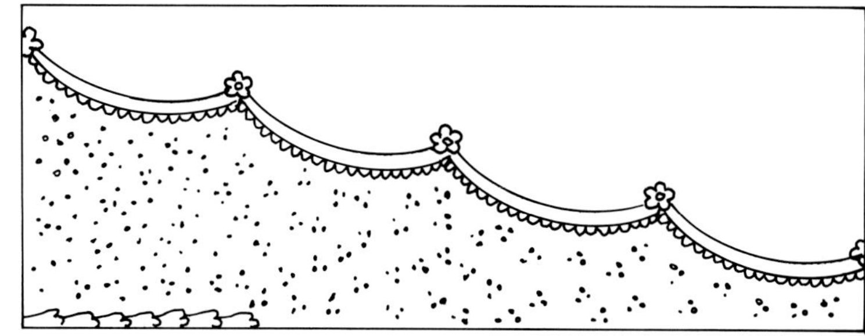

Shell border

Garland of roses and leaves using piping, mould or ejector cutter in contrasting colour.
Loops using No. 0 tube in same colour as cake.

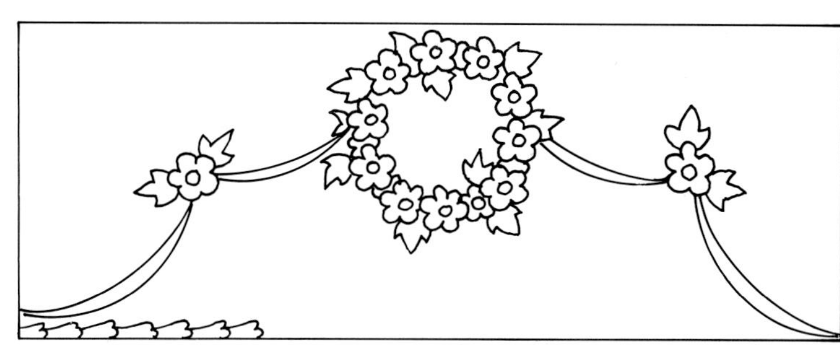

Shell border

True lover's knot made with forget-me-nots using piping, mould or ejector cutter in contrasting colour.
Loops using No. 0 tube in same colour as cake.

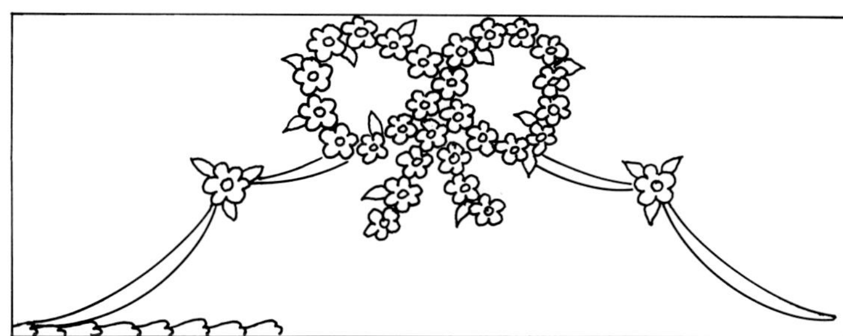

Small trail border

Loops and lattice using No. 0 tube in same colour as cake.
Flowers using piping, mould or ejector cutter and leaves in contrasting colour.

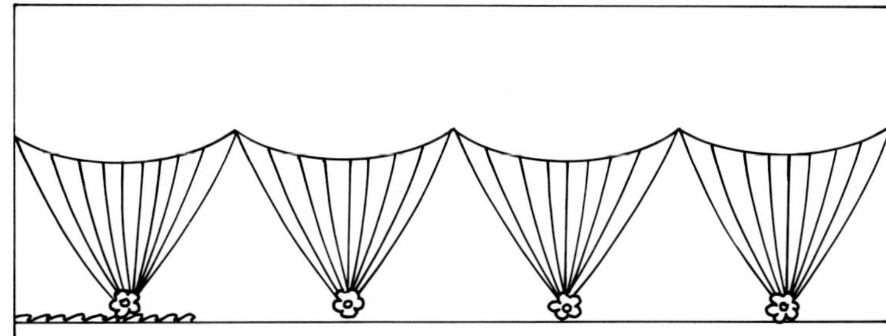

Shell border

Loops using No. 0 tube in same colour as cake.
Forget-me-not flowers using ejector cutter in contrasting colour.
Border using No. 4 or 5 tube.

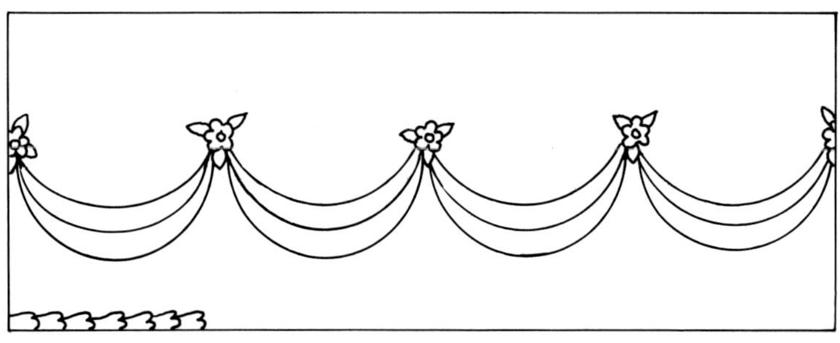